Things You Can Do

How to **FIGHT CLIMATE CHANGE** and **REDUCE WASTE**

Written by
Eduardo Garcia

Illustrated by
Sara Boccaccini Meadows

TEN SPEED PRESS
California | New York

Contents

Introduction

> "The greatest threat to our planet is the belief that someone else will save it."
>
> — **ROBERT SWAN**, British explorer and the first person to walk to both poles

Are you familiar with the parable of the hummingbird? It goes like this:

One day, a huge wildfire breaks out in the forest, forcing all the animals to flee. Terrified, they find refuge by the edge of the forest, where they feel overwhelmed and helpless as they watch the ferocious flames destroy their beautiful home. They are paralyzed, except for the hummingbird, who says, "I'm going to do something about this fire." She flies to the nearest river, scoops a few drops of water with her beak, rushes toward the blaze, and drops the water onto the fire. And off goes the hummingbird, back and forth between the river and the flames at whizzing speeds, dropping water into the blaze at every turn. The rest of the animals are stupefied. The elephants, the bears, the deer, and the other big critters that could carry much more water yell at the hummingbird, "What are you doing? Your beak is tiny, you can barely carry any water!" And without missing a beat, the hummingbird turns around and tells them, "I'm doing the best I can."

That's what *Things You Can Do* is about—doing the best we can.

Like the forest animals in the hummingbird parable, we're facing our biggest challenge as greenhouse gases warm our planet, wreaking havoc on the climate system. Earth's average surface temperature has risen by around 2.1°F (1.2°C) since the start of the Industrial Revolution. The extra heat has thrown the climate system off balance, unleashing catastrophic events, from rising sea levels and destructive mega-storms that threaten coastal communities to wildfires that turn billions of trees into ash and droughts that deplete fertile cropland of nutrients.

The reason is clear. Greenhouse gases, like carbon dioxide, are trapping the sun's heat in the atmosphere. We humans have created all that carbon dioxide by burning fossil fuels with our cars, our airplanes, our factories, and our power plants.

The solution is clear, too. We need to stop burning fossil fuels and usher in a green economy that relies on renewable energy, electric and shared forms of transportation, and sustainable diets.

But that is easier said than done. For decades, those with the most power to fight climate change have turned a blind eye. Politicians, company executives, and investors have mostly stayed on the sidelines, watching this catastrophe unfold, issuing targets that they rarely meet, and even denying that climate change is happening at all.

AFTER DECADES OF BROKEN PROMISES, EXPECTING THAT GOVERNMENTS AND CORPORATIONS WILL FIX THE CLIMATE CRISIS IS AT BEST NAIVE AND AT WORST IRRESPONSIBLE AND RECKLESS. WE NEED TO DEMAND THAT THEY IMPLEMENT TRANSFORMATIVE CHANGES TO SLASH EMISSIONS, BUT IT'S ALSO UP TO US, THE HUMBLE HUMMINGBIRDS, TO DO THE BEST WE CAN.

And there is a lot we can do. Research cited by the United Nations shows that households are responsible for two-thirds of greenhouse gas emissions, which makes sense when you consider that there are 7.7 billion people on Earth—and by 2050 we will be nearly 10 billion.

But we are not all equally responsible. Those of us living in the United States, the European Union, and other developed countries have greater carbon footprints because we typically drive bigger cars and have to heat and cool larger homes with electricity generated by burning fossil fuels. To compound the problem, the food we eat is mostly produced by industrial farms that cause deforestation and rely on aggressive agrochemicals that poison pollinators and pollute waterways. And we generate humongous amounts of waste, much of which ends up in the environment, where it kills countless animals.

There is no question about it—our lifestyles are destroying planet Earth. Like parasites, we live at the expense of our host.

But we can turn things around. If each one of us reduces the carbon emissions associated with our lifestyles, it will go a long way toward fighting climate change.

This book was inspired by a series of stories I wrote for the *New York Times*. Beautifully illustrated by Sara Boccaccini Meadows, backed by peer-reviewed research, official statistics, and interviews with researchers and activists, *Things You Can Do* is a toolbox filled with dozens of actionable tips that will allow you to slash your carbon footprint and live in closer harmony with nature. From reducing plastic waste, recycling efficiently, and increasing your car's mileage to cooling your home without an air conditioner, composting, and eating a climate-friendly diet, this book is packed full of thoughtful practices and ideas that can build a bridge to a better tomorrow.

ONE

There Is No Planet B

Earth is the most magical place in the universe. It's the only planet where countless species of plants and animals have flourished through millennia, from single-cell organisms like cyanobacteria to mighty dinosaurs and everything in between.

They have all thrived here for the simple reason that Earth is the only planet in our solar system with the right temperature to sustain life. That temperature is constantly changing—it varies with the seasons, drops at nighttime, and is influenced by the weather.

The temperature also depends on where on Earth you are. Equatorial regions remain warm most of the year, and the poles tend to be pretty cold all the time.

The coldest place on Earth is Vostok, Antarctica, where the thermometer dropped to −128.6°F on July 21, 1983.

The highest temperature of 134°F was recorded in Death Valley, California, on July 10, 1913.

By measuring temperatures in many places across the globe and through the years, scientists have come up with an average surface temperature for the period 1951 to 1980: 57°F.

That is pretty balmy—perfect for life to thrive.

That's in large part because Earth is in the so-called Goldilocks zone. Our planet is not too close to its host star (the sun) and not too far—just the right distance for liquid water to exist. If we were closer, water would evaporate. If we were farther away, it would freeze.

Earth is also perfect for life because the liquid metal in its core works with the planet's rotation to generate a magnetic field that keeps gases trapped in the atmosphere. If it weren't for this magnetic field, those gases would be spilled into space.

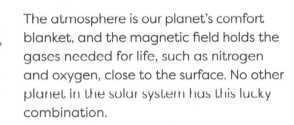

The atmosphere is our planet's comfort blanket, and the magnetic field holds the gases needed for life, such as nitrogen and oxygen, close to the surface. No other planet in the solar system has this lucky combination.

The Solar System's Gas Giants

Jupiter. The largest planet in the solar system, Jupiter is twice as massive as all the other planets combined and is thought to have 79 moons. Jupiter is made mostly of swirling gases and liquids, with an atmosphere of hydrogen and helium. Its powerful atmospheric pressure turns the hydrogen into liquid, creating the largest ocean in the solar system. Jupiter cannot sustain life because it does not have a solid surface and is beset by ferocious storms that can last for centuries—the planet's Great Red Spot is an anticyclonic storm that has lasted for at least 340 years.

Saturn. Named after the Roman god of agriculture and wealth, Saturn is a massive ball of mostly hydrogen and helium. It is encircled by seven rings made of chunks of ice, rock, and as many as 82 moons. Saturn is also unlivable. The strongest hurricane on Earth can reach a top wind speed of 360 feet per second, while the winds in Saturn's upper atmosphere reach 1,600 feet per second. The atmospheric pressure of Saturn is so powerful that it turns gas into liquid, just like on Jupiter. Astronomers think that two of its moons, Enceladus and Titan, could potentially host microbial life.

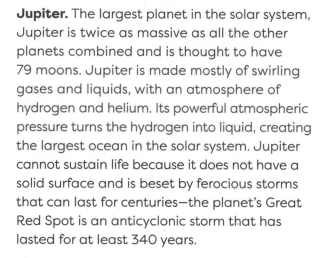

Uranus. Named after the Greek god of the sky, Uranus was the first planet to be discovered with the aid of a telescope. It has 13 faint rings and 27 small moons. Uranus has a rocky core, but most of its mass is a hot, dense mix of icy materials like water, methane, and ammonia. It has an atmosphere composed of hydrogen and helium, with a small amount of methane that makes it look blue. Uranus can't support life as we know it because conditions there are too extreme and volatile. Near its core, temperatures can reach 9,000°F, but Uranus has the coldest atmosphere of any planet in the solar system.

Neptune. The most distant planet of our solar system, Neptune is 30 times farther from the sun than Earth. Like Uranus, Neptune is also composed mainly of water and ammonia with traces of methane wrapped around a small rocky core. Astronomers think there might be an ocean of superhot water under Neptune's icy atmosphere. Life as we know it is not possible on Neptune. The average temperature there is about −331°F, and its atmosphere is volatile, with winds that whip clouds of frozen methane across the planet at around 1,200 miles per hour—faster than a supersonic jet.

The Solar System's Rocky Planets

Mercury. As the smallest planet and the closest to the sun, Mercury can get pretty hot, with daytime temperatures reaching 800°F. At night, though, temperatures can drop to −290°F, because Mercury's atmosphere is too thin to retain heat. It's composed mostly of oxygen, sodium, hydrogen, and helium atoms blasted from the surface of the planet by the constant bombardment of asteroids, debris from comets, and the solar wind.

Venus. The second planet from the sun, Venus is similar in size to Earth. It has no moons or rings and is peppered by tens of thousands of volcanoes. Like Uranus, Venus rotates in the opposite direction of Earth: from east to west. Its thick atmosphere is composed mainly of carbon dioxide—a greenhouse gas that traps heat underneath—making Venus the hottest planet in the solar system. Surface temperatures can reach 900°F, hot enough to melt lead. The extreme heat and the toxic atmosphere make Venus inhabitable.

THE SOLAR SYSTEM ALSO HAS FIVE DWARF PLANETS (CERES, PLUTO, ERIS, HAUMEA, AND MAKEMAKE), MORE THAN 1.1 MILLION ASTEROIDS, AND MORE THAN 3,700 COMETS.

Earth. Whereas all the other planets are named after Greek and Roman deities, Earth comes from a Germanic word that means "the ground." The oceans cover 70 percent of Earth's surface and hold 97 percent of its water. The planet's land features dynamic landscapes that include mountains, canyons, volcanoes, and valleys. Our planet has an atmosphere that is responsible for the long-term climate and short-term local weather, and it keeps us warm and cozy by retaining heat underneath. Life has flourished here. Cyanobacteria, butterflies, baobabs, gray whales, panda bears, owls, emperor penguins, tardigrades, daffodils, zooplankton—an estimated 8.7 million species of plants, animals, and microorganisms call planet Earth home. Scientists have only identified 14 percent of them.

Mars. About half the size of Earth, Mars features a rugged surface that has been altered by volcanoes, meteor impacts, dust storms, and plate tectonics. Mars has an atmosphere made up mostly of carbon dioxide, nitrogen, and argon. It is 100 times thinner than Earth's and not very effective at trapping heat underneath. As a result, temperatures can vary rapidly, going from 70°F to −225°F. Mars can't sustain life because it is too cold and too dry there, but astronomers think that conditions were friendlier to life eons ago. Features that resemble river and lake beds show that there was once liquid water on the surface of Mars.

The Sun

The sun is the primary source of energy on Earth. Our star transfers heat through radiation (radiate means to send out or spread from a central location). This radiation is carried from the sun, which is 93 million miles away, to our planet by electromagnetic waves in about eight and a half minutes.

The radiation that is visible is called visible light, but there are other types of solar radiation that we can't see, such as ultraviolet light, infrared, microwaves, radio waves, X-rays, and gamma rays.

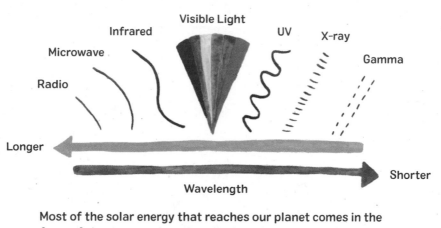

Most of the solar energy that reaches our planet comes in the form of shorter wavelength radiation.

About 30 percent of the solar energy that reaches our planet is reflected back into space by the atmosphere, the Earth's surface, and the ice caps through what is known as the albedo effect. (*Albedo* is another word for reflectivity—white surfaces reflect more solar energy than darker ones.) About 19 percent is absorbed by the atmosphere and clouds, and 51 percent reaches the land and the oceans, warming them.

Sun

6% scattered from atmosphere

**20% scattered and
reflected by clouds**

**19% absorbed by
atmosphere and clouds**

**4% reflected
by surface**

51% absorbed by the Earth

The Earth's surface then releases that energy in three ways:

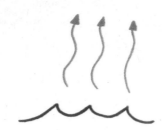

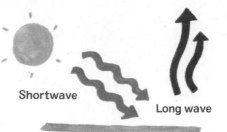

Shortwave

Long wave

Water evaporation. The sun's energy turns water into its gaseous state, generating clouds and contributing to all kinds of weather phenomena, including rain and snow.

Radiation. Most of the solar energy that reaches our planet comes in the form of shortwave radiation but is transformed into heat and then released by the Earth's surface as longer-wavelength infrared radiation.

Conduction and convection. These are the twin engines of our planet's weather. Conduction is a transfer of heat by direct contact: the Earth's surface releases the solar energy that it has absorbed into the air. Because that air is now warmer, it raises up and passes on the heat to other gas molecules through a process called convection.

The energy that the Earth releases is equal to the amount of solar energy that reaches the surface of our planet. In other words, the energy that drives our planet is governed by the first law of thermodynamics, which states that energy cannot be created or destroyed, just transformed.

But, in actuality, the amount of solar energy that stays on our planet depends largely on the atmosphere.

The Atmosphere

Earth's atmosphere is a wonderful thing. It acts as a natural thermostat that regulates our planet's temperature, letting in just the right amount of radiation from the sun, while releasing most of the extra heat that bounces from the surface of the planet out into space.

Our atmosphere shields the planet from impacts of small and medium-sized meteors, which often burn upon coming into contact with atmospheric gases. It also contains a layer of ozone that protects our planet's surface from harmful ultraviolet radiation.

The atmosphere is composed of:

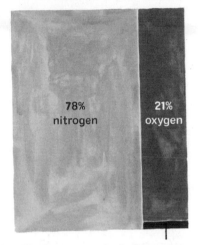

78% nitrogen

21% oxygen

1% other gases—including argon, helium, methane, and carbon dioxide

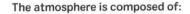

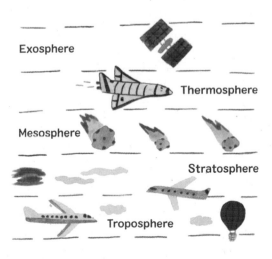

Exosphere

Thermosphere

Mesosphere

Stratosphere

Troposphere

Earth's atmosphere extends for about 300 miles and has five layers: the troposphere, stratosphere, mesosphere, thermosphere, and lastly, the exosphere.

Most atmospheric gases are concentrated in the troposphere, the layer closest to the surface, and most of the weather happens in this 7-mile-thick layer.

Weather and Climate

Weather is the state of the atmosphere at a particular place and time. When we discuss the weather, we mean how hot or cold it is in our town today, for example, or whether it will be humid or dry, calm or windy, clear or cloudy. Climate, on the other hand, refers to the average atmospheric conditions over longer periods of time. In regions with a tropical monsoon climate, for example, temperatures are fairly steady throughout the year, and heavy rains come only during certain months.

Climate is often described as the average weather in a particular region over more than 30 years. While the weather can change rapidly, climate changes very slowly.

The movement of water between the atmosphere and the ground is called the water cycle. This is how it works: The sun evaporates large amounts of water from oceans, rivers, lakes, and other water bodies. As it rises, the water vapor expands and cools, and clouds develop. When air becomes saturated with moisture, droplets form. When these droplets grow large enough in size, they fall toward the ground as rain.

The troposphere contains aerosols, small particles that can travel long distances by hitching a ride on wind currents. They include dust, sand particles, spores, volcanic ash, and pollen. Aerosols also include sulfur particles from the burning of fossil fuels—especially low-quality coal—and many are the result of car exhausts and industrial pollution. Europe and the U.S. began phasing out cheap coal in the 1970s and 1980s, after it was discovered that sulfur emissions cause acid rain. China and India, countries that depend heavily on coal for power generation, are now the top emitters of sulfur dioxide.

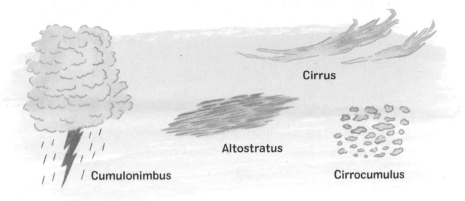

At any given time, **clouds** cover about two-thirds of the Earth and vary from fair-weather cirrus to towering cumulus clouds. Clouds bring snow to the Alps, downpours to the Amazon jungle, summer storms to your local park, and much-needed water to the crop fields that grow our food.

The troposphere contains an average of 37.5 quadrillion gallons of water vapor—enough to cover the entire surface of the planet with 1 inch of rain.

Weather and climate are also driven by other factors. Earth tilts on its axis about 23.5 degrees. That's the reason why sunlight reaches different parts of the planet more directly at different times of the year, creating the seasons. Because Earth is round, the tropics absorb more energy than the polar caps. As warm air along the equator moves upward, colder air from neighboring areas rushes in to fill the void, creating currents that move hot air from the equator toward the poles. Meanwhile, the Earth's rotation causes some of these winds to rotate toward the west near the equator.

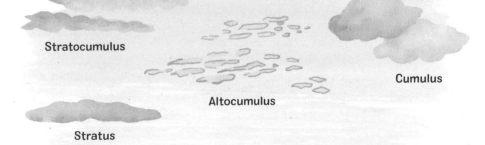

Greenhouse Gases

When it comes to keeping our planet cozy and warm, most of our atmosphere plays no role. Nitrogen and oxygen, for example, are transparent to incoming solar radiation and outgoing infrared radiation. It is naturally occurring greenhouse gases—water, carbon dioxide, methane, and nitrous oxide—that keep Earth warm.

Without them, Earth's average temperature would be near 0°F instead of the much warmer 57°F. But too much of a good thing can be a bad thing. Whenever greenhouse gases increase, the temperature of our planet goes up.

- -

Water (H_2O). As the most abundant greenhouse gas, water vapor plays a major role in regulating air temperature because it absorbs solar energy and thermal radiation from the planet's surface. The atmospheric water vapor concentration varies from trace amounts in the poles to nearly 4 percent in the tropics, but it's thought to be increasing as more water evaporates from the oceans due to higher temperatures in the lower atmosphere.

Carbon dioxide (CO_2). Carbon dioxide is naturally present in the atmosphere as part of the Earth's carbon cycle—the natural circulation of carbon among the atmosphere, oceans, soil, plants, and animals. But carbon dioxide is also a waste product that results from the burning of fossil fuels (coal, oil, and natural gas) and the manufacturing of cement, steel, iron, and plastic. Carbon dioxide is removed from the atmosphere when it is absorbed by plants through photosynthesis. That's why deforestation is a key contributor to climate change.

Methane (CH_4). When it comes to its greenhouse gas effect, methane is 25 times more powerful than carbon dioxide, but it only stays in the atmosphere for about a decade; carbon dioxide typically stays for at least 100 years. Although methane is naturally produced by microbes called methanogens, research indicates that about 60 percent of global methane emissions are the result of human activities, including

KEY GREENHOUSE GASES EMITTED BY HUMAN ACTIVITIES

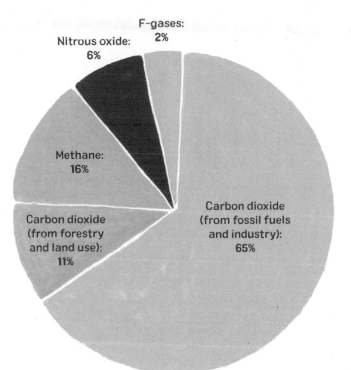

F-gases: 2%

Nitrous oxide: 6%

Methane: 16%

Carbon dioxide (from forestry and land use): 11%

Carbon dioxide (from fossil fuels and industry): 65%

the production and transport of fossil fuels, raising livestock, agriculture, and the decomposition of organic waste in landfills.

Nitrous oxide (N_2O). Nitrous oxide is produced naturally by chemical processes that occur in the oceans and on land. Nowadays, however, it's also released into the atmosphere when farmers around the world apply synthetic fertilizers to their crops. Other sources of nitrous oxide include the combustion of fossil fuels and the treatment of wastewater. When it comes to retaining heat, nitrous oxide molecules are 300 times more powerful than carbon dioxide.

Fluorinated gases (F-gases) are man-made greenhouse gases that include hydrofluorocarbons, perfluorocarbons, sulfur hexafluoride, and nitrogen trifluoride. They are synthetic, powerful greenhouse gases that come from the manufacturing of certain products—mainly refrigerants used to make air conditioners (ACs) for buildings and cars. They are emitted in small quantities, but because they have a potent greenhouse effect and sometimes stay in the atmosphere for thousands of years, fluorinated gases are referred to as High Global Warming Potential gases.

Fossil Fuels and Greenhouse Gases

Plants harness the sun's energy through photosynthesis and use that energy to grow. When they wither and die, that energy is conserved in their carbon-rich remains. With the passing of millions of years, those remains transform due to the heat and pressure to which they are subjected in the Earth's crust, turning into fossil fuels—namely oil, coal, and natural gas.

Humans have been burning fossil fuels to produce energy and power our transportation systems since the start of the Industrial Revolution in the mid-1700s. The burning of fossil fuels releases greenhouse gases into the atmosphere. Since the advent of the Industrial Revolution, atmospheric concentrations of carbon dioxide, methane, and nitrous oxide increased by 49 percent, 162 percent, and 23 percent, respectively.

ATMOSPHERIC CONCENTRATIONS
OF GREENHOUSE GASES

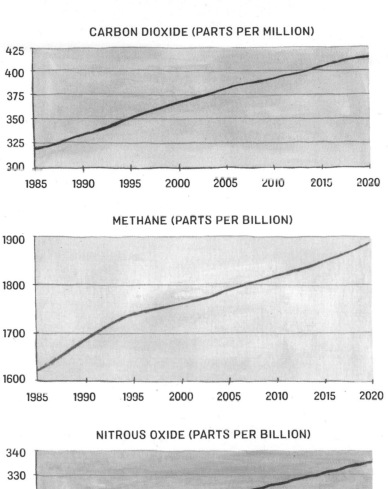

CARBON DIOXIDE (PARTS PER MILLION)

METHANE (PARTS PER BILLION)

NITROUS OXIDE (PARTS PER BILLION)

Let's look at carbon dioxide, which is responsible for about two-thirds of the energy imbalance that causes climate change. During the past 250 years, the carbon dioxide concentration has jumped to nearly 415 parts per million molecules of air, roughly 50 percent more than before the Industrial Revolution.

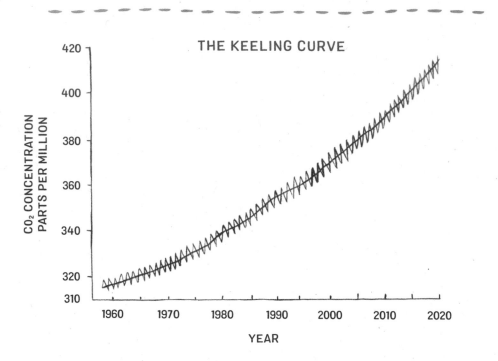

THE KEELING CURVE

The Keeling Curve is named after Charles David Keeling, who started measuring the atmospheric concentrations of carbon dioxide at the Mauna Loa Observatory on Hawaii in 1958. His data show two things. First, carbon dioxide levels follow a seasonal rhythm: They decrease after the spring in the Northern Hemisphere, when plant growth removes carbon dioxide from the air through photosynthesis, and increase in the winter due to plant decay. Second, over the long term, carbon dioxide is becoming more prevalent in the atmosphere. That long-term surge correlates with the rapid increase in greenhouse gas emissions.

MORE GREENHOUSE GASES = MORE HEAT BEING TRAPPED IN THE LOWER ATMOSPHERE = HIGHER TEMPERATURES

Our planet is warming; the evidence is clear and overwhelming. In 2014, a group of 1,300 international scientific experts concluded that there is more than 95 percent probability that human activities during the past 50 years have warmed our planet.

Since the 1880s, the Earth's average temperature has increased by around 2°F (1.2°C), with approximately two-thirds of that warming occurring in the last handful of decades. According to the United Nations, 1983 to 2012 was likely the warmest 30-year period of the last 1,400 years. All seven years from 2014–2020 were the hottest on record globally.

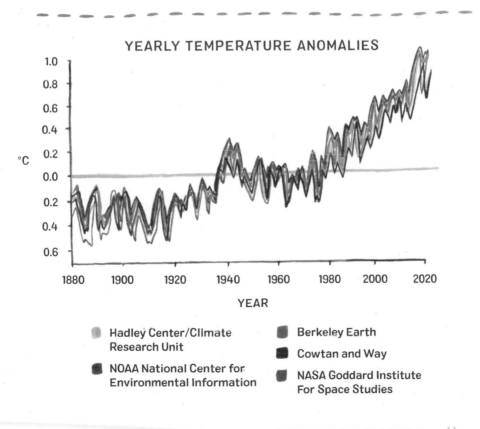

YEARLY TEMPERATURE ANOMALIES

Hadley Center/Climate Research Unit

NOAA National Center for Environmental Information

Berkeley Earth

Cowtan and Way

NASA Goddard Institute For Space Studies

The Climate Crisis

This extra heat is unleashing a string of devastating events across the world.

Wildfires. Drier areas are more vulnerable to wildfires. Western Europe, California, Alaska, Chile, and Siberia have been hit by destructive wildfires in recent years. In 2019 and 2020, wildfires in Australia razed 50 million acres of land, killing 34 people and millions of animals—including koalas, wallabies, wombats, and kangaroos—and destroying 6,000 homes and other structures. Insects that thrive in warmer temperatures have killed hundreds of millions of trees in the U.S. and Canada in recent years, turning them into kindling for devastating wildfires.

Heat waves. Climate change is making heat waves more than twice as likely to occur in some places. In recent years, severe droughts linked to climate change have occurred in southern Africa, Australia, Brazil, the U.S., and Europe. Some of them have lasted for years. High temperatures reduce soil moisture, which often leads to food shortages because we depend on fertile soils for the vegetables, grains, and fruit we consume, as well as for livestock feed.

Flooding. Warmer air tends to hold more moisture, which can bring more frequent and intense rainfall to some areas. Heavier rains cause streams, rivers, and lakes to overflow, which damages lives and property and can contaminate drinking water. Flooding is expected to increase in densely populated urban areas near rivers and the coast. In the U.S., more flooding is already occurring in the Mississippi River Valley, Midwest, and Northeast.

Mass extinctions. Earth is facing its sixth mass extinction. Meteorites and massive volcano eruptions were largely to blame for previous mass extinctions, but this one is being caused by human actions, and climate change is a contributing factor. Researchers say that about a third of all plants and animal species may go extinct in the next five decades. Many species are struggling to adapt to the changing climate. The timing of natural events such as flowering and egg-laying is shifting. Some species, like Chinook salmon and the monarch butterfly, are changing their migration patterns, and animals such as mackerel and bumblebees are being forced to find new habitats.

Storms. Hurricanes, typhoons, and cyclones get their energy from the temperature difference between the warm ocean waters and the cold upper atmosphere. Because that temperature difference will be more marked going forward, powerful storms will be more frequent and intense. Instead of occurring every 100 years, mega-storms like Hurricane Harvey are expected to strike every 16 years.

Ocean acidification. The oceans absorb about a third of the carbon dioxide that humans are releasing into the atmosphere. When carbon dioxide mixes with saltwater, chemical reactions occur that make the water more acidic. This is having a marked impact on marine life, especially mollusks, crabs, and corals. In combination with higher water temperatures, acidification has triggered bleaching events that killed around 50 percent of corals in Australia's Great Barrier Reef in 2016 and 2017. Researchers estimate that between 70 and 90 percent of coral reefs worldwide will likely die by 2040.

Melting ice caps. Temperatures in the Arctic are rising twice as fast as anywhere else on Earth. In June 2020, the temperature reached 100.4°F in the Arctic Circle, the highest value ever recorded there. The increased heat is melting the polar ice caps as well as permafrost—ground that is continuously frozen. When it melts, permafrost releases carbon dioxide and methane into the atmosphere, aggravating climate change. Mountain glaciers on which millions of people rely for drinking water and irrigation are also disappearing.

Sea level rise. The global sea level has risen by about 8 inches since 1880 and is expected to rise another 1 to 4 feet by 2100. This is the result of added water from melting land ice and thermal expansion, as water expands when it warms up. Sea level rise, storm surges, and high tides are forecast to displace more than 600 million people from coastal areas by the end of the century. Rising sea level is also damaging agricultural land across the world, especially near densely populated river deltas in Asia, and threatens the survival of people living in small island nations like the Maldives.

The Warming Trend

Scientists say that all these extreme events will become more frequent and much more severe if our average temperature rises by 2.7°F (1.5°C) above pre-industrial levels. If that occurs, climate change will probably be irreversible.

The carbon budget is the amount of carbon dioxide that the world can emit while still keeping the global temperature from rising more than 2.7°F (1.5°C). Estimates vary, but in 2018 the United Nations Intergovernmental Panel for Climate Change put that number at 420 billion metric tons of carbon dioxide, which is approximately 10 years' worth of emissions. In other words, if emissions continue at the current rate, we will reach that threshold by 2030, if not earlier.

THE CARBON BUDGET FOR 1.5°C

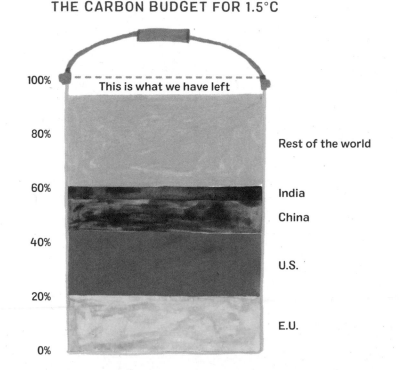

This is what we have left

Rest of the world

India

China

U.S.

E.U.

Greenhouse Gases by the Numbers

GLOBAL GREENHOUSE GAS EMISSIONS BY ECONOMIC SECTOR

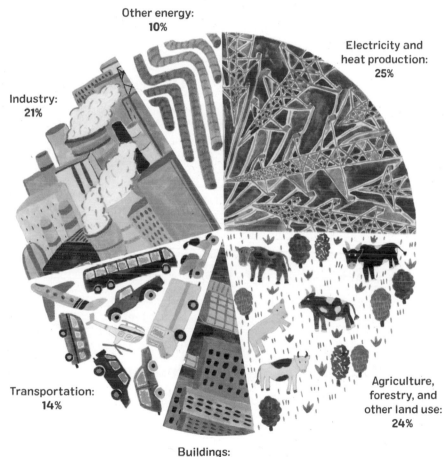

Other energy: 10%

Electricity and heat production: 25%

Industry: 21%

Transportation: 14%

Agriculture, forestry, and other land use: 24%

Buildings: 6%

But Who Is Responsible?

Historically, the U.S. is the country with the highest greenhouse gas emissions. China, however, currently dumps more carbon dioxide into the atmosphere than any other country because its huge industrial sector depends heavily on coal for power generation.

CUMULATIVE CO_2 EMISSIONS FROM 1750–2019 IN BILLION METRIC TONS

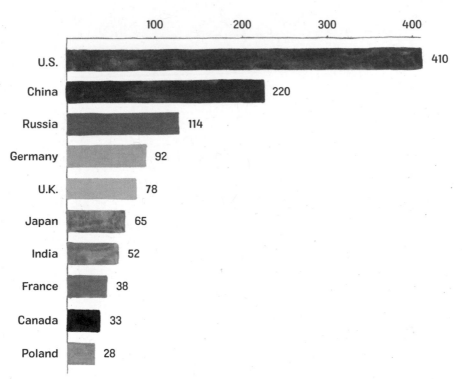

U.S.	410
China	220
Russia	114
Germany	92
U.K.	78
Japan	65
India	52
France	38
Canada	33
Poland	28

Over the past few years, carbon dioxide emissions have been increasing in China and other rapidly growing countries, while they have been more or less steady in industrialized nations.

CO₂ EMISSIONS FROM FOSSIL FUEL USE IN 2020
34.1 billion metric tons*

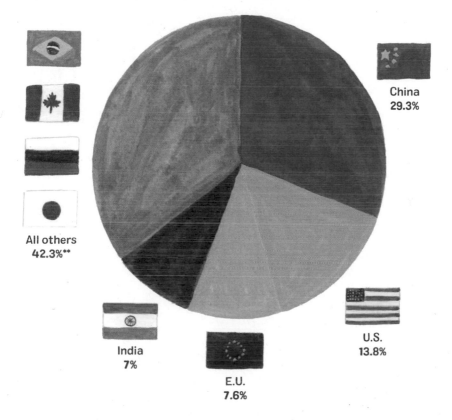

China
29.3%

All others
42.3%**

India
7%

E.U.
7.6%

U.S.
13.8%

* In 2020, emissions dropped slightly due to the economic slowdown caused by the COVID-19 pandemic.

** All others include emissions from international aviation and maritime navigation bunker fuels.

The Carbon Footprint

Carbon is shorthand for all the different greenhouse gases that contribute to climate change, and *footprint* describes the impact that something has on the environment. The carbon footprint, therefore, measures the amount of greenhouse gases that each person puts into the atmosphere. The cars we drive, the electricity that cools and warms our homes, the food we eat, and the things we throw away cause greenhouse gas emissions.

Carbon footprints differ depending on your location and lifestyle choices, but there is a clear correlation between income and carbon emissions. People who earn more money emit more greenhouse gases because they drive larger cars, have bigger homes, and buy more food. Worldwide, the wealthiest 10 percent of people are responsible for nearly half of the total global emissions.

That's why people living in wealthier countries have a larger carbon footprint. For instance, the average carbon footprint for a person living in the United States is more than 16 metric tons per year, one of the highest rates in the world and four times the global average.

ANNUAL CO$_2$ EMISSIONS
FROM FOSSIL FUEL USE PER CAPITA

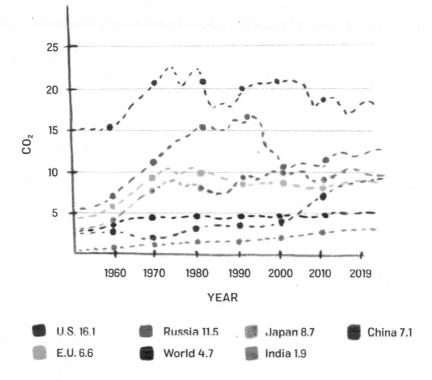

CO$_2$

25
20
15
10
5

1960   1970   1980   1990   2000   2010   2019

YEAR

- U.S. 16.1
- Russia 11.5
- Japan 8.7
- China 7.1
- E.U. 6.6
- World 4.7
- India 1.9

Individual carbon footprints add up to a lot. About **two-thirds** of global emissions are linked to household consumption and lifestyle choices.

TO ENSURE THAT TEMPERATURES DON'T RISE ABOVE THE 2.7°F (1.5°C) THRESHOLD, EACH ONE OF US NEEDS TO REDUCE OUR INDIVIDUAL CARBON FOOTPRINT TO AROUND 2.5 METRIC TONS BY 2030. GOVERNMENTS AND COMPANIES SHOULD HELP US DO THAT, BUT THEIR INACTION MEANS THAT MUCH OF THOSE REDUCTIONS COME DOWN TO OUR OWN LIFESTYLE CHANGES.

No Time to Lose

Scientists say that we face a dystopian future . . . unless we decrease greenhouse gas pollution by 45 percent from 2010 levels by 2030 and reach net zero emissions by 2050.

"Solving the climate crisis is the greatest and most complex challenge that Homo sapiens has ever faced. The main solution, however, is so simple that even a small child can understand it. We have to stop our emissions of greenhouse gases. . . . Either we prevent 1.5°C of warming or we don't. Either we avoid setting off that irreversible chain reaction beyond human control or we don't. Either we choose to go on as a civilization or we don't. That is as black or white as it gets. There are no grey areas when it comes to survival."

—GRETA THUNBERG, Swedish climate activist

"Climate change is life or death. We could be accused of being alarmist, but if we have faith in science, then something very serious is happening. Climate change and global warming is the new global battlefield. It is being presented as if it is the problem of the developed world. But it's the developed world that has precipitated global warming."

—WANGARI MAATHAI, Nobel laureate and founder of the Green Belt Movement

"It doesn't make any sense that if you think we are the most intellectual creature on the planet that we're destroying our only home. I truly believe that we have a window of time that is closing. If we get together during that window of time, we can start to heal some of the harm we have inflicted or at least slow down the climate crisis."

—JANE GOODALL, English primatologist

"We tend to forget that it is humans who have caused climate change, and we tend to export responsibility to large corporations or governments. The fact is, we all contributed to it. If we all reduce our emissions, collectively we give a signal to the market."

—CHRISTIANA FIGUERES, founder of Global Optimism and head of the UN Climate Change Conference held in Paris in 2015

"In the twenty years since I first started talking about the impact of climate change on our world, conditions have changed far faster than I ever imagined. It may sound frightening, but the scientific evidence is that if we have not taken dramatic action within the next decade, we could face irreversible damage to the natural world and the collapse of our societies. We're running out of time, but there is still hope."

—DAVID ATTENBOROUGH, English broadcaster, naturalist, and author

- - -

TWO

Power Up

We started burning fossil fuels to produce electricity in 1882, when Thomas Edison built the first coal-fired commercial power station in London. Fast-forward 140 years, thousands upon thousands of thermal power plants have been built all over the world. Nowadays, facilities that burn fossil fuels produce most of the electricity we use to heat and cool our homes and power scores of devices, from computers and TV sets to refrigerators and washing machines.

But things are changing. Renewable energy is growing quickly, and environmentally conscious citizens are finding myriad ways to slash the amount of electricity they use at home, helping reduce our dependence on fossil fuels for power generation.

Fossil Fuels and Electricity

About two-thirds of the electricity generated worldwide is produced by burning coal, natural gas, and oil in thermal power stations. Whatever fossil fuel they use, thermal plants rely on two devices to generate electricity: turbines and generators.

STEAM TURBINE

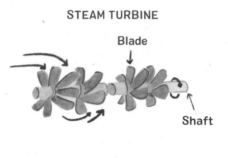

Blade

Shaft

This is how these plants work: When coal, natural gas, and oil are burned, they heat up water in a boiler. When that water evaporates, it produces steam, and that steam moves the blades of a turbine. The turbine then moves an electromagnetic generator that transforms the kinetic energy into electrical energy.

ELECTROMAGNETIC GENERATOR

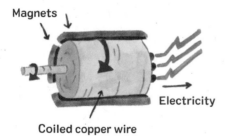

Magnets

Electricity

Coiled copper wire

The first electromagnetic generator, the Faraday disk, was invented in 1831 by British scientist Michael Faraday. Although it was very inefficient, the Faraday disk demonstrated that it was possible to generate electricity using magnetism.

Today, approximately 80 countries generate power by burning coal, up from 66 in 2000. Global coal use nearly doubled between 2000 and 2019.

THERMAL POWER PLANT

Located in the Inner Mongolia Autonomous Region of China, the Datang Tuoketuo Power Station is the world's biggest coal-fired power plant.

The James H. Miller Jr. Power Plant in Alabama is the largest coal plant in the U.S. and also the country's top emitter of greenhouse gases.

Each plant emits more carbon dioxide than Kenya, a country with a population of more than 50 million people.

Coal Hungry

THE WORLD'S FIVE MOST POPULATED COUNTRIES PRODUCE MUCH OF THEIR POWER BY BURNING COAL

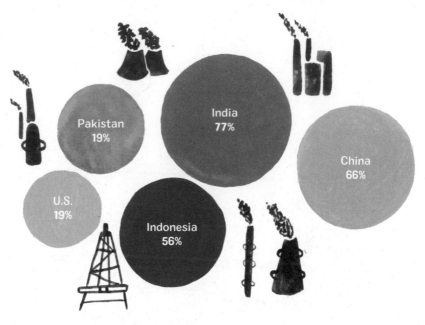

Coal is used to generate approximately 40 percent of the world's electricity.

The amount of carbon dioxide that coal-fired power stations emit depends on how efficient they are and the type of coal they burn, but they typically emit around 50 percent more carbon dioxide than plants that burn natural gas and 50 to 100 times more than nuclear, wind, or solar power stations.

To keep the global temperature increase below the 2.7°F (1.5°C) threshold, coal use has to decrease by at least 80 percent over the next decade. However, experts say that coal power generation will likely continue steadily over the next few decades. Although the U.S., the E.U., and the U.K. are phasing out coal, rapidly growing countries that need cheap electricity, such as Vietnam, Indonesia, and Turkey, plan to build new coal-fired power stations.

COAL IS THE ENEMY

GLOBAL ELECTRICITY GENERATION
BY SOURCE

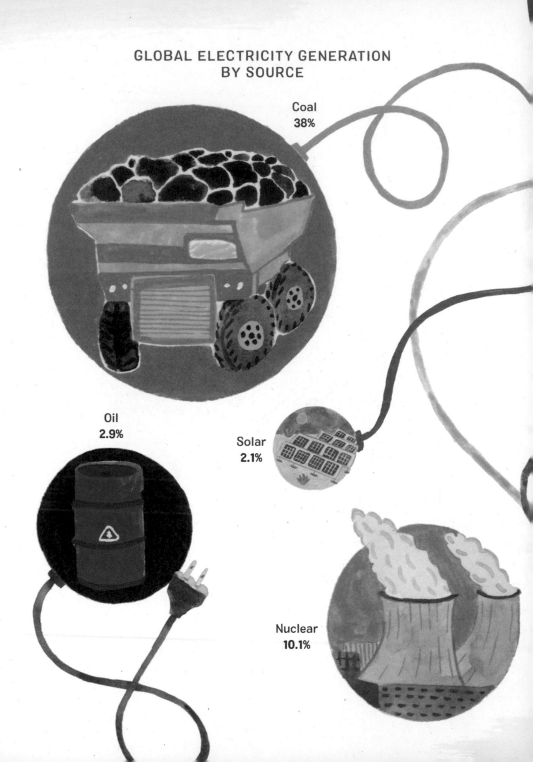

Coal
38%

Oil
2.9%

Solar
2.1%

Nuclear
10.1%

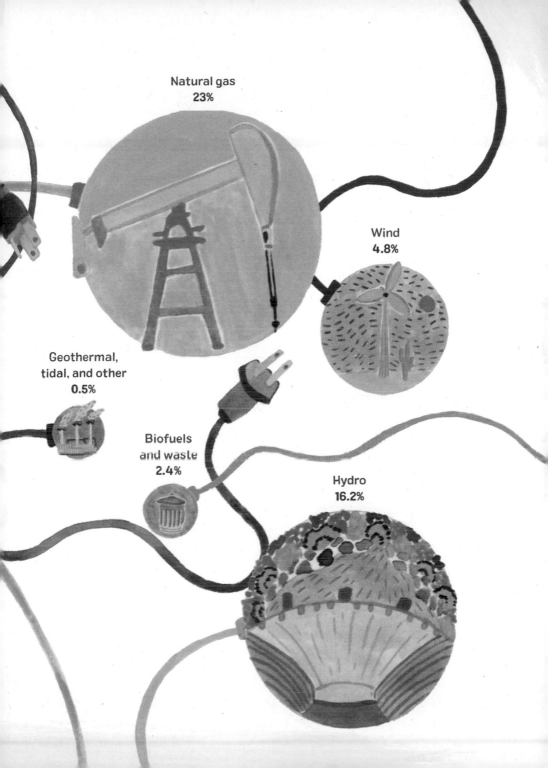

Natural gas
23%

Wind
4.8%

Geothermal,
tidal, and other
0.5%

Biofuels
and waste
2.4%

Hydro
16.2%

Electricity Powers Modern Life

The electricity generated by power companies is mainly used to manufacture products and run appliances at home. Global electricity consumption grows at a faster rate than population, meaning that people are increasingly using more electricity.

GLOBAL ELECTRICITY CONSUMPTION BY SECTOR

Industrial
42%

Residential
26.9%

Commercial and public services
21.5%

Transportation
1.7%

Other
7.9%

Electricity and Carbon Emissions

In 2019, the average US home used 10,649 kilowatt-hours of electricity, generating 7.5 metric tons of carbon dioxide, which is the equivalent of:

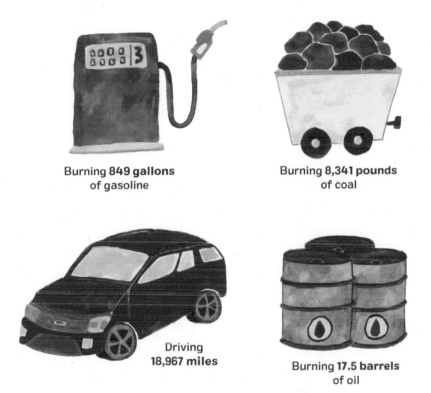

Burning **849 gallons** of gasoline

Burning **8,341 pounds** of coal

Driving **18,967 miles**

Burning **17.5 barrels** of oil

US household electricity usage is more than twice the per capita consumption in the European Union and almost four times as much as the global average. That's in large part because Americans tend to have larger homes that are often not well insulated and also due to the prevalence of ACs.

Electricity at Home

About 20 percent of global carbon emissions come from the energy we use at home. These are the major uses:

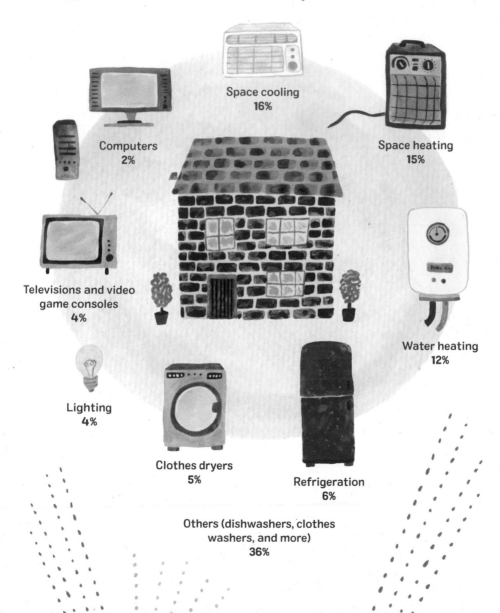

Space cooling
16%

Computers
2%

Space heating
15%

Televisions and video
game consoles
4%

Water heating
12%

Lighting
4%

Clothes dryers
5%

Refrigeration
6%

Others (dishwashers, clothes
washers, and more)
36%

Light Bulbs

There are dozens of different bulbs on the market, but most household bulbs belong to one of these four categories:

Incandescent bulbs were the only choice until the 1980s. These bulbs are highly inefficient, though, because they convert most of the energy they use into heat instead of light.

Compact fluorescent bulbs have become popular in recent decades and do a much better job at using energy efficiently. The latest versions use up to 75 percent less energy than incandescent bulbs.

Halogen bulbs became available in the 2000s. They are about 30 percent more efficient than incandescent bulbs and can last ten times longer.

Light-emitting diodes (LEDs) are the best choice because they use up to 85 percent less energy. A 10-watt LED delivers as much light as a 60-watt incandescent bulb and can last up to 25 years.

Using more efficient light bulbs can help us prevent the burning of fossil fuels. If Americans were to replace all their incandescent and halogen lamps with LEDs, it would prevent more than 30 million metric tons of carbon emissions every year.

Air Conditioners Are Power Hogs

ACs are very popular. In the U.S., nearly 90 percent of homes have one. AC adoption is also high in Japan (90 percent) and Australia (72 percent). In Europe, however, only around 20 percent of homes have one.

Wherever you live, using less air-conditioning will help you lower your carbon footprint because ACs consume a lot of power and discharge hot air that can raise outside temperatures. It's a catch-22: the more we use ACs, the hotter it gets.

With heat waves becoming more frequent and urban populations on the increase, the use of energy-hungry ACs is set to surge. By 2050, worldwide energy demand for space cooling is expected to triple. Since most of the world's electricity is generated by burning fossil fuels, the increased use of ACs will lead to higher carbon dioxide emissions.

To make matters worse, ACs use hydrofluorocarbon, a potent greenhouse gas that often ends up in the atmosphere during the manufacturing, installation, and disposal of AC units.

Although there are places where life would be unbearable without them, the truth is that ACs are often overused.

NOT ALL ACs ARE MADE EQUAL

Buying the right AC will help you shrink your emissions and save on your electricity bill.

By and large, AC units fall into four different categories (see facing page). The best choice depends on your budget and whether you need to cool down a room or a whole house.

Portable ACs are designed for small spaces. Overall, they are less efficient than other options but can be a valid choice for those who don't have the right windows or are on a tight budget.

Ductless mini-split ACs can also cool down a small part of the house. Though they are expensive, they are easy to install and can also provide heating.

Central ACs are more efficient and more expensive, suitable for those who need to cool a large family home. The latest models use 30 to 50 percent less energy than older ones, so upgrading could be a good idea, especially if your central AC is decades old.

Window ACs are not very efficient, but they are the best choice to cool a room or a small apartment, especially if used sparingly. If you go for a window AC, make sure that it is the right size for your space—choosing one that is too big would waste energy. Also, make sure you secure it well, using duct tape to seal possible leaks.

Whatever AC you choose, do your research to ensure that you're buying the most efficient one. Many countries have efficiency labels for domestic appliances.

In the U.S., look for the Energy Star label—Energy Star ACs are more efficient than standard models.

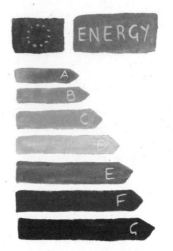

In Europe, efficiency labels rate appliances from A to G.

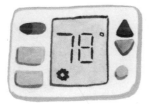

If you already have an AC, the most important thing you can do is to use it sparingly. Set the thermostat to 78°F when you are at home and need cooling. Raise the thermostat a few degrees when you leave your home, especially if you plan to be out for a few hours, and at night, when your body temperature drops.

Things You Can Do
to cool down your home without an AC

Install a ceiling fan. A ceiling fan uses very little energy and can help cool a big room.

Use a box fan. A well-placed box fan can bring relief from the heat. When positioned next to a window at night, it can inject cool air into your home. Remember to shut fans down when you leave—fans cool people, not homes.

Remove rugs during the hotter months. This will help your place feel cooler.

Draw your curtains when the sun is high to help keep the heat out.

Take advantage of the wind. Open your windows when the sun is down to let the breeze in. Opening several windows at the same time creates a refreshing current.

Buy sheets and clothes made with natural materials, such as cotton or linen. These fabrics allow you to stay cool because they are more breathable than synthetic alternatives.

Avoid using the oven in the summer. It radiates a lot of heat.

Invite in some plants. By absorbing humidity and providing shade, houseplants can help cool your home.

Around and Around

Revolving doors save energy because they help buildings stay warm in the winter and cool in the summer. If all buildings have revolving doors and everybody uses them, we will be able to reduce emissions by saving energy.

Things You Can Do
to lower energy consumption in the winter

Adjust the thermostat. Set your thermostat to 68°F while you're awake and set it lower while you're asleep or away from home—but not much lower, because keeping the temperature consistent helps save energy.

Bundle up. Use blankets, scarves, and thick socks for extra wintertime warmth.

Let the sunshine in. Open your curtains to get free heat during the day, but close them at night to keep the heat in and the cold out.

Set ceiling fans to turn clockwise. Since heat rises, this pulls cooler air upward to the ceiling and pushes warmer air downward.

Keep internal doors closed, especially if there are parts of your house that you don't use.

Don't block the heat. A bulky piece of furniture next to the radiator will absorb the heat.

If you bake, leave the oven door open when you finish to utilize the extra heat.

Things You Can Do
to keep the heat in

Make sure your windows are tightly closed.

Put up some curtains. When drawn at night, curtains can help prevent around 10 percent of a room's heat loss. If you live in a very cold area, you could install thermal-insulated curtains.

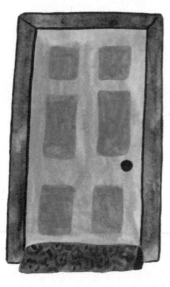

Place a draft stopper under the door. This is a great way to ensure that heat stays in a room.

Seal your home's ductwork. Check around the ducts in your attic, basement, and garage and place some mastic sealant or metal tape around any gaps you discover.

Caulk and weather-strip your home. Chances are the heat escapes mostly through cracks around your windows.

Weatherize Your Home

Many homes are not prepared for the winter. Small holes and cracks in your window frames, around the corners of your AC unit, behind moldings, and under baseboards may be letting cold air in, increasing your heating bill and your carbon footprint. Experts say that if you were to add up all the various gaps, the average US home would have a 3 by 3-foot hole in the wall. But finding all those small holes can be challenging. For that, homeowners need to get an energy audit, a service that some utility companies provide for free.

Vampire Power

On average, American homes contain 65 devices that draw power even when they are switched off. That's the case for many TV sets, laptop computers, gaming consoles, cable boxes, printers, cordless phones, coffee makers, microwave ovens, dishwashers, heated towel racks, electric toothbrush chargers, and laundry machines.

While idle, on standby, or in sleep mode, these devices consume 50 large (500-megawatt) power plants' worth of electricity every year. If you unplug most of them, you could potentially reduce your home's greenhouse gas emissions from electricity generation by around 5 percent. Using a smart power strip is a good way to ensure that these appliances don't draw power when they are not being used. You can also use timers or smart outlets, which have a switch to completely cut out power.

Eduardo's Toilet Hack

When I was seven or eight years old, I noticed a few tiny pieces of gravel at the bottom of the toilet. I told my mother, and she promptly lifted the lid of the toilet's tank to show me where the gravel came from. You see, for most of my childhood, my mother kept a football-size rock inside the toilet tank.

This may sound crazy, but she knew what she was doing. There were three kids and two adults in our household, and each one of us flushed the toilet several times a day. That's a lot of water going literally down the toilet. At one point, my mother realized that by hacking the toilet we would be using significantly less water, saving a small fortune in our water bill, and helping conserve dwindling water resources. And the toilet worked just fine.

The largest use of household water is the toilet, followed by showers and baths. In 2009, researchers estimated that carbon dioxide emissions related to extracting, transporting, and treating water for US households were equivalent to the annual greenhouse gas emissions of 53 million passenger vehicles.

Things You Can Do
to save water and energy at home

Turn down the refrigerator. Don't run your fridge on the maximum setting, and try to keep the doors open as little as possible. If you don't buy a lot of food, get a small fridge; you may be wasting energy cooling a lot of empty space.

Use cold water and sunshine for the laundry. Not using hot water to wash clothes saves significant amounts of energy; if you're washing lightly stained clothes, chances are that cold or luke-warm water will work just fine. If you have a backyard, try drying clothes on a clothesline instead of using the dryer.

Run your dishwasher only when full. You can also experiment with the shorter run time settings— often, the speed wash setting gets dishes plenty clean. If washing your dishes by hand, soak them first in a dish bin. This will allow you to significantly reduce your water use.

Fix leaks. A leaky faucet that drips at the rate of one drip per second can waste thousands of gallons of water per year. Installing a faucet aerator can help you reduce your tap's flow by around 40 percent.

Install a more efficient showerhead. This can save up to 2,700 gallons of water per year. Singing in the shower can be fun, but sticking to short songs helps save water and the energy used to heat that water.

Put a lid on it. Cooking with the lid on and using a pot that matches the size of your burner will help you save energy.

50 CENTS

Green Energy Times

VOL. No. 5214   Green Energy Times   MONDAY, MARCH, 22, 2025

THE RENEWABLE ENERGY REVOLUTION IS HERE

GREEN POWER SOARS!

Renewable energy generation capacity grew by 10.3 percent in 2020, faster than fossil fuel and nuclear power combined. Overall, clean energy now accounts for nearly 37 percent of the total installed power generation capacity worldwide.

RENEWABLES REACH NEW RECORD IN THE US

The United States produced nearly 20 percent of its electricity from renewables in 2020. The administration of President Joe Biden aims to reduce carbon emissions from the energy sector to zero by 2035.

INDONESIA SAYS NO TO COAL

Indonesia generates around 60 percent of its power by burning fossil fuels, but its government is betting on renewables. The Southeast Asian country plans to replace up to 69 old coal-fired power stations with renewable energy plants.

COMPANIES TURN THEIR BACKS ON FOSSIL FUELS

eBay (2025), H&M (2030), Target (2030), and Walmart (2025) have pledged to source all their power from renewables soon. Google, Apple, and Facebook already source 100 percent of their electricity from renewables.

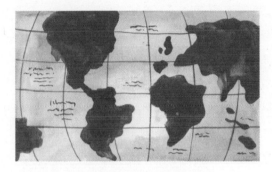

INVESTORS DROP FOSSIL FUELS

Norway's $1.1 trillion fund, the world's largest sovereign wealth fund, has unveiled plans to invest billions of dollars in wind and solar power projects. The fund also plans to withdraw $8 billion in investments in 134 companies that explore for oil and gas.

AMBITIOUS TARGETS DRIVE GREEN ENERGY GROWTH

Countries, regions, cities, and towns around the world have set ambitious renewable energy targets. California aims to produce 60 percent of its electricity from renewable resources by 2030 and 100 percent by 2045. The European Union's renewable energy target is 32 percent by 2030. Latin America has pledged to produce 70 percent of its power from renewables by that year. Iceland, Paraguay, and Costa Rica already produce virtually all of their electricity from renewables.

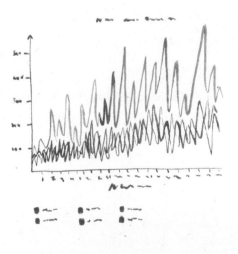

The Future Is Renewable . . .

RENEWABLE ENERGY GENERATION BY ENERGY SOURCE IN 2020

Hydropower 43% | Wind 26% | Bioenergy **4.5%**

Solar 26% | Geothermal and marine energy **0.5%**

Worldwide, there are about 60,000 large dams, making hydropower the largest source of renewable energy. Hydroelectric dams rely on turbines and generators to turn the kinetic energy of the water into electricity, while also holding water for drinking and irrigation. In 2018, the Itaipu Hydroelectric Dam supplied 15 percent of the electricity consumed in Brazil (population 210 million) and 90 percent of the energy consumed in Paraguay (population 7 million).

Photovoltaic solar is the fastest-growing renewable energy source. Solar farms rely on panels fitted with many photovoltaic cells that transform solar energy into electricity. The price of solar panels is coming down, and they are becoming increasingly efficient: New bifacial solar panels feature photovoltaic cells on both the top and bottom. The top cell captures the sun's energy, and the bottom one absorbs light reflected off the ground. Bifacial panels generate 15 to 20 percent more power than one-sided solar panels.

El Romero, in Chile's Atacama Desert, is one of the largest photovoltaic solar plants in Latin America. It generates an average of 493 gigawatt-hours of electricity a year, enough clean energy to power 240,000 homes. A coal power station with that capacity would emit 474,000 metric tons of carbon dioxide every year, whereas El Romero emits none.

. . . And It's Already Here

Wind power has been harnessed by humans for millennia. Our ancestors used windmills to grind grains and transfer water for irrigation. Today, we use wind turbines to produce clean energy. Turbines in onshore wind power stations typically have a production capacity of 2 to 5 megawatts, enough to power hundreds of homes. Offshore turbines can generate 12 megawatts, and future models under development will be able to generate 15 megawatts.

Bioenergy is created with organic materials from plants and animals. In a typical biomass power plant, wood chips and agricultural waste are burned to heat up pipes filled with water. The water then turns into steam, and the steam drives a turbine that turns a generator that produces electricity. The Polaniec Biomass Power Plant in southern Poland is the world's largest biomass power plant. It produces enough electricity to power 320,000 homes.

Geothermal comes from the Greek words for "earth" and "heat." Geothermal stations produce clean energy by injecting water into pipes to a depth of around 2 miles. The heat of the Earth turns the water into steam, which is transformed into electricity using a turbine and a generator. Italy's Larderello is the oldest geothermal plant in the world. The first generator was installed there in 1904, and a power plant started producing energy for customers in 1913. The Larderello complex now features 34 geothermal plants that collectively produce enough power for 2 million homes.

Tidal energy is in our near future. MeyGen is set to be the world's first major tidal energy project; it is situated off Scotland's northernmost coast at a site called Pentland Firth, which has some of the planet's most powerful tidal currents. MeyGen currently relies on four underwater turbines to produce enough electricity for 2,600 homes. The plan is to add dozens of turbines over the next few years. Scientists estimate that the Pentland Firth strait could provide enough electricity to cover half of Scotland's power needs.

Buy Green Energy

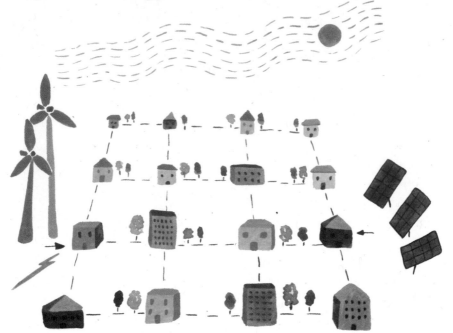

A great way to reduce your carbon footprint is to buy clean energy for your home. Unfortunately, that's easier said than done. Only countries with a liberalized energy market allow consumers to choose where their power comes from. In the U.S., only about 18 states have liberalized electricity markets.

But regardless of the state you live in, you can always buy Renewable Energy Certificates. Each one represents a given amount of electricity that's been generated from renewable sources, so when you buy a Renewable Energy Certificate, you ensure that a renewable energy company gets paid for the power you consume. The more people buy these certificates, the more money renewable energy companies will earn.

The Power of the Sun

The most effective way to harness the sun's energy is to install solar panels on your roof. In the U.S., a typical home installation will set you back an average of $12,000 after federal tax incentives, not including any state tax benefits. It's a hefty sum, but panels often pay for themselves in about seven years.

You can also join forces with your neighbors through community solar, which refers to members of a community coming together to build a small solar plant.

Wahleah Johns

Cofounder of Native Renewables, a company that aims to supply off-grid solar systems to 15,000 families in the Navajo Nation

According to traditional knowledge, the sun plays a powerful role in helping our people overcome challenges and hardships. There is a strong cultural connection in every indigenous tribe and nation; we all have narratives about the role of the sun, but also the moon and water and land and fire. We abide by the natural laws, and we pray to nature. We pray because if it weren't for nature, we wouldn't be here, so we have to give thanks.

Many of our tribal members live in rural communities where they are far from the power grid. It's hard to extend a transmission line to their homes. We see off-grid solar as a good solution to that problem because we get over three hundred days of sunlight in the Southwest. Solar panels complement who we are as indigenous people.

An off-grid solar system can generate enough power for a refrigerator and sustainable lighting and electronics. Panels can last over twenty years if they're well taken care of, and customers know how to use their energy efficiently. Education is key. We can't just leave on the lights or plug in a space heater all day. We have to turn off appliances. It's a behavioral shift.

When we install a system, we see how it makes a difference for the families. Many families are able to have a refrigerator for the first time, and they can keep their food cold and don't have to feed themselves with canned food, which means they eat more healthily. They can also power a water pump that allows for indoor plumbing, which is a game-changer. They can also have access to the internet.

A fridge, indoor plumbing, and internet access. These families don't have the three things that we take for granted in the U.S. It's disheartening, but when they get off-grid solar, there is a powerful shift. A real improvement. With time, they become self-reliant and self-sustainable.

"In Navajo Nation, we have fifteen thousand families that don't have access to electricity. If we can get them off-grid solar, they could be the model for how we should be living in the world."

- - - - -

THREE

A Climate-Friendly Diet

F ood is Earth's gift to us. Once upon a time, humans were hunter-gatherers, but we later learned to harness those wild gifts by domesticating plants and animals. Over time, humans have seized 37 percent of the planet's land surface to grow crops and feed livestock, while destroying forests and pushing many wildlife species to extinction.

Nowadays, industrial farming relies on tilling, monocultures, and toxic agrochemicals to produce food for the planet's 8 billion people. Food production accounts for a quarter of our carbon emissions. By 2050, there will be 10 billion of us. By then, food demand is expected to increase by 50 percent, putting increased pressure on the environment.

But there is hope. We can turn things around by saying no to animal products, eating a climate-friendly diet, buying from sustainable farms, and slashing food waste.

Food Production and Climate Change

The meals that at least half of the world's population eat come mostly from industrial farming, a system that relies on monocultures to grow staples such as soy, corn, and wheat.

The origins of industrial farming go back to the early 1900s, when a German chemist named Fritz Haber figured out a method to produce ammonium nitrate, the main ingredient of both synthetic fertilizers and explosives. Synthetic fertilizers contain a handful of nutrients that help plants grow, including nitrogen, phosphorus, potassium, and sulfur.

Once upon a time, these nutrients were provided by microbes such as bacteria, fungi, and protozoa that were naturally present in the soil. These microbes live in a symbiotic relationship with plants, helping them flourish. But pesticides and tilling are killing these microorganisms. On top of that, industrial farmers don't let their land rest between growing seasons, which further damages the soil.

That's bad news because healthy soils naturally store the carbon absorbed by plants through photosynthesis. When soil microbes die, they release that carbon into the atmosphere. And when synthetic fertilizers are applied, soils release nitrous oxide—a potent greenhouse gas.

Industrial farmers also apply pesticides and herbicides to ensure that insects and weeds don't damage their crops. These agrochemicals are toxic to pollinators, including bees, bats, butterflies, and hummingbirds, which help plants reproduce by passing pollen from flower to flower.

Decades of agrochemical use, in combination with other intensive farming practices, kill the upper layers of the soil, which are rich in organic matter and minerals. When topsoil dies, farmland gradually becomes barren because it no longer holds the nutrients on which plants feed. As the world's population continues growing, demanding increasing amounts of food, farmers are cutting down forests in search of more fertile land.

The Meat Industry Is a Greenhouse Giant

Whether it's turkey on Thanksgiving, a burger on Saturday night, or bacon for breakfast, humans have come up with countless ways to eat meat. There's nothing wrong with that. The problem is that we eat too much of it. Globally, people eat an average of almost 75 pounds of meat every year. In industrialized nations, however, people eat twice as much. To produce all that meat, the food industry raises billions of cows, pigs, and chickens every year. To make space for that livestock, humans have encroached on the habitat of wild animals. The result is that wild animals are disappearing at an incredibly fast pace.

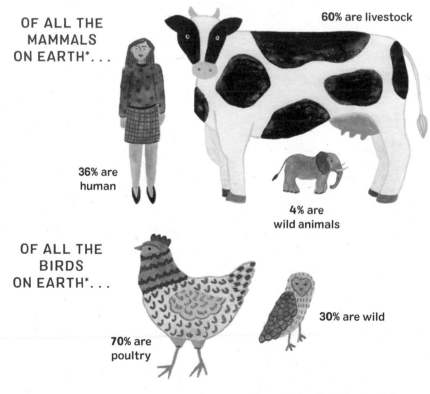

OF ALL THE MAMMALS ON EARTH*...

60% are livestock

36% are human

4% are wild animals

OF ALL THE BIRDS ON EARTH*...

70% are poultry

30% are wild

as a percentage of the Earth's total biomass

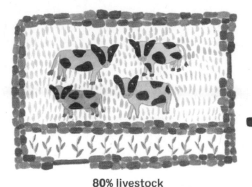

Farmed animals need much more land and water than plants, even though they don't provide us with nearly as many nutrients.

18% calories
37% protein

80% livestock

Nearly **80 percent** of all agricultural land is for livestock. But livestock produce just **18 percent** of the food calories and **37 percent** of the protein that humans eat. And livestock account for at least **15 percent** of our greenhouse gas emissions.

95% of methane expelled

5% of methane expelled

Manure is also a source of both methane and carbon dioxide.

Much of those emissions come from belching cows. Belching is due to a digestive process called enteric fermentation, by which microbes in a cow's digestive tract convert sugars from the food it eats into smaller molecules that can be absorbed into its bloodstream. A byproduct of this process is methane, which the cow expels mostly by burping—and a bit through flatulence.

Animal Food

After cow methane emissions, the production of animal feed is the second-largest source of emissions for the livestock sector. To raise cows, goats, pigs, and chickens, farmers need to constantly clear land for pasture and to grow crops to feed the animals. Livestock feed comes mainly from corn and soybeans, and producing it contributes to a range of problems linked to industrial agriculture, including greenhouse gas emissions—nitrous dioxide from the use and production of fertilizers and carbon dioxide from deforestation. About one-third of the world's cropland is used to grow crops for animal feed.

FEED REQUIRED TO PRODUCE 1 POUND OF . . .

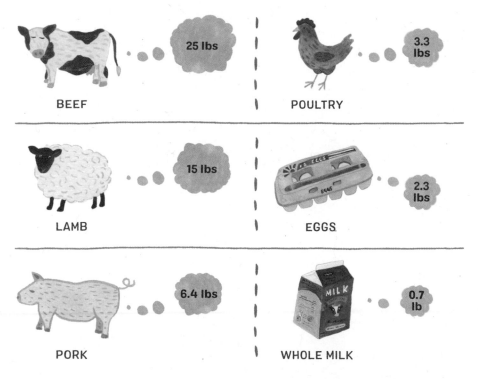

25 lbs — BEEF	3.3 lbs — POULTRY
15 lbs — LAMB	2.3 lbs — EGGS
6.4 lbs — PORK	0.7 lb — WHOLE MILK

In order to increase profits, the livestock industry keeps animals confined in small spaces.

Chickens and turkeys are often kept in cages so small that they cannot even extend their wings. The cages are inside huge sheds that are often windowless and have so little fresh air that they need to be artificially ventilated.

Cows are social animals that enjoy gathering in herds and grazing in rolling grasslands. However, the dairy industry keeps them in cramped indoor spaces, sometimes tied to individual stalls to hold them in place or inside stanchion barns, where they are restrained in a head yoke while they rest, milk, and eat. Dairy producers sometimes inject cows with growth hormones to increase milk production.

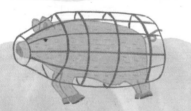

Pigs lead miserable lives. Male pigs are castrated to stop them from producing hormones that would give pork meat a bad taste. They are often confined in enclosures so small that they cannot even turn around. Antibiotics are often used to help animals survive these unhealthy living conditions, contributing to rising rates of antibiotic resistance and the loss of precious medicines for humans.

Beef cattle typically spend the first few months of their lives in open grasslands before being moved to feedlots. Once there, they are fed grains and concentrates, which their stomachs struggle to digest, causing health problems. After they put on a few hundred pounds, they are sent to the slaughterhouse.

FOOD: GREENHOUSE GAS EMISSIONS
ACROSS THE SUPPLY CHAIN

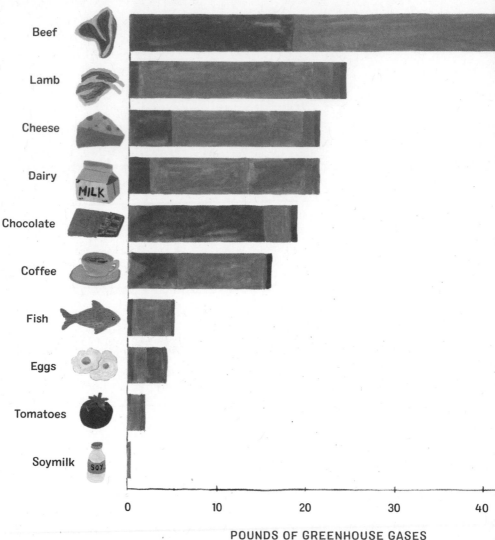

POUNDS OF GREENHOUSE GASES
PER POUND OF PRODUCT

Meat and dairy have the highest carbon footprint of all food products, and they are responsible for more biodiversity loss and water consumption than their alternatives. But not all meat is made equal. Eating beef, lamb, and cheese is the equivalent of burning coal to produce energy. Chicken and pork are responsible for much fewer emissions—but they are still very high when compared to those of fruit and vegetables.

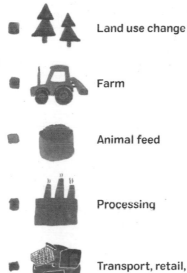

Land use change

Farm

Animal feed

Processing

Transport, retail, packaging

50   60

Things You Can Do
to eat fish in a sustainable way

Sustainable Fish

Fish is not only delicious, it has a much smaller environmental footprint than meat and plenty of nutrients—like iron, zinc, and omega-3 fatty acids—that are hard to find in other food products. But when it comes to their environmental footprint, not all fish are made equal.

Choose fish with abundant stocks. There is not enough fish in the wild to sustain the fast-growing human population, in part because humans have overfished some species. Larger predatory species like Atlantic salmon, Atlantic cod, snapper, tuna, and shark tend to be overfished, so it's a good idea to stay away from them. If you like tuna, go for skipjack tuna, which is more abundant than yellowfin or bluefin.

Choose fish whose populations are well managed, like Alaskan wild salmon and Alaskan pollock, for example.

Choose cold water Maine lobster. This fishery is managed sustainably, whereas lobster from elsewhere may have been fished from areas where their numbers are in rapid decline.

Read the fine print. Shrimp sold in supermarkets come mostly from farms, with China, Vietnam, and Ecuador being the world's top exporters. Some shrimp are farmed using sustainable methods, but others are not.

Buy your fish from producers that have obtained an eco-certification. Sometimes wild fish like cod, tuna, and octopus are harvested from depleted stocks or using methods that impact fish habitats or incidentally kill or injure other species, including marine mammals.

Purchase fish species that are lower down on the food chain. Forage fish such as mackerel, anchovies, herring, and sardines are more abundant because they have not been as heavily targeted as larger fish.

Buy farmed mollusks. Most oyster reefs have disappeared due to overfishing, so wild oysters are a no-no. Wild mussels and clams are sometimes sourced sustainably, but their numbers are also decreasing in some areas. When it comes to oysters, mussels, and clams, the best choice is to buy those produced in sustainable farms, where mollusks help restore the marine environment by filtering water while creating habitat for crabs and fish.

ATLANTIC COD

ATLANTIC SALMON

RED SNAPPER

HERRING

ANCHOVY

ATLANTIC MACKEREL

CLAMS

OCTOPUS

SKIPJACK TUNA

POLLOCK

SQUID

SARDINE

OYSTERS

MUSSELS

WILD SHRIMP

LOBSTER

Small Fisheries and Eco-Labels

To ensure that the wild fish you buy has been harvested from healthy stocks and using methods that cause minimum damage to the marine ecosystem, buy products certified by the **Marine Stewardship Council**, which are available in more than 100 countries.

By 2030, two-thirds of all of the seafood we eat will come from aquaculture—up from around half at present. That's good because, by and large, aquaculture can enable the creation of more seafood without putting greater pressure on wild fish stocks, and farmed seafood has a much lower carbon footprint than livestock. Be it salmon, tilapia, mollusks, or prawns, look for the **Best Aquaculture Practices** (BAP) and the **Aquaculture Stewardship Council** (ASC) eco-labels to ensure that farmed seafood has been raised in a sustainable way.

As a rule of thumb, small local fisheries can be a smart environmental choice, especially in industrialized countries, where strict regulations force small-boat fishermen to catch fish using sustainable methods. It helps if customers are open to trying different fish. That allows small boat fishermen to catch whatever is abundant at a particular time of the year.

Although people worldwide eat thousands of fish species, most super-markets offer no more than ten types of fish. If we were to eat more species, we wouldn't be putting all the pressure on just a handful of species and pushing them to the brink of extinction. To broaden your horizons, shop at a fishmonger. If you buy a whole fish, rather than just a boneless, skinless fillet, you will ensure that no additional resources are used to prepare your meal and that as little as possible gets wasted.

Things You Can Do
to eat a more climate-friendly diet

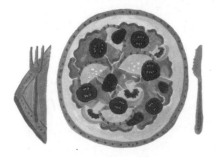

Go vegan. The main dietary change that will help you reduce your carbon footprint is to eschew animal and fish products altogether. If we all switched to a vegan diet, global greenhouse gas emissions from food production would be slashed by 58 percent. People in the U.S., Brazil, Argentina, and Australia eat more meat than the average global citizen; if they became vegans, it would reduce their carbon footprints even more dramatically.

Become a flexitarian. A flexitarian eats meat every now and then, but it's the exception, not the rule. Consider taking red meat off the menu completely—replacing it with chicken and turkey will help lower your emissions.

Opt for the two-thirds plan. If you feel the need to eat meat more frequently, fill your plate with two-thirds foods like vegan burger patties and sausages, whole grains, fruits, vegetables, nuts, and legumes and one-third with animal products. When it comes to animal products, look for small fish and mollusks that have a much smaller environmental footprint than meat. Choosing plant-based meals more often than not will go a long way toward reducing your carbon emissions.

Reduce dairy as much as possible. Vegan cheeses have become mainstream, and there are plenty of delicious options. Replace milk with a nondairy alternative, but know that not all vegan milks are made equal: when it comes to their environmental footprint, oat and soy are preferable to coconut, almond, and rice milks.

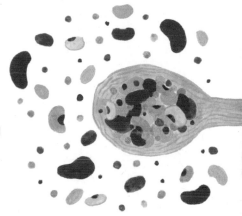

Meet your new friend, the pulse! Worldwide, we need to triple consumption of beans, lentils, and peas and eat four times more nuts and seeds in order to slash emissions. If we substitute protein-rich pulses for meat and eggs, farmers will grow more of these edible seeds. That's good for the environment because pulses fertilize the soil by drawing nitrogen from the atmosphere, and good for us because pulses are rich in protein, vitamins, complex carbohydrates, and fiber. Plus, there are some delicious products made with pulses like tofu, hummus, falafel, and peanut butter!

Avoid refined grains, highly processed foods, and drinks with added sugars. All of these products have a larger carbon footprint than fresh fruits and vegetables and are less healthy for you.

Diversify your diet. Eating a wide variety of foods will ensure that your body gets all the nutrients it needs while encouraging farmers to grow different crops in small plots instead of one single crop in a huge plot.

Many of us should eat less. Worldwide, **2 billion adults** are overweight or obese, and most of them are in industrialized countries.

If we ate smaller portions, less food would be produced, allowing us to free cropland for new forests.

The Carbon Footprint of Pet Food

There are around 900 million dogs and 600 million cats worldwide. That's *a lot* of hungry animals. And the numbers are increasing rapidly as people in emerging countries become more affluent and can afford to have pets.

We typically feed pets kibble, which is made by mixing plant-based carbohydrates with byproducts from the meat industry, such as liver, kidneys, and spleen, all of which are highly nutritious but don't have much demand among humans. This type of pet food has a relatively small carbon footprint because those byproducts might otherwise end up in a landfill.

But some upmarket pet meals use human-grade ingredients like chicken breast or pork loin. These meat cuts have a greater environmental impact because, to produce them, farmers need to raise more livestock. In turn, this livestock requires land, water, and additional animal feed.

Things You Can Do

to ensure your furry friends enjoy a diet that is healthy for both them and the planet

Choose products that contain proteins from plants, chicken, or fish. Pet foods that are rich in beef have a large environmental footprint. Cats are strictly carnivores, but dogs are omnivores and may do well on a diet that has more plant protein.

Buying pet food that contains organic and non-GMO ingredients can also help.

Leftovers from our own meals are also a good option.

Also, bear in mind that obesity is pretty common among pets in Western countries. More than half of the roughly 135 million cats and dogs in the U.S. are overweight or obese. That's unhealthy, both for our furry friends and the planet.

Organic Food = Lower Emissions

There is no doubt that by using huge quantities of fertilizers, herbicides, and pesticides, industrial farms harm the environment. Organic farmers, however, skip agrochemicals and thereby help protect soil microorganisms and pollinators. Buying products from small organic farmers can help us reduce our carbon footprint because crops grown using sustainable methods draw carbon dioxide from the atmosphere and store it in soils. In addition, when nitrogen-based fertilizers are applied to cropland, soils release huge quantities of nitrous oxide, a major greenhouse gas.

GMOs and Herbicides

Organic food can't include GMOs, organisms that have had their genetic code modified. Biotechnology companies tweak the DNA of crops like corn and soy to make them resistant to herbicides—that way when herbicides are applied, they kill weeds but not the crops. Powerful herbicides like glyphosate, the world's best-selling weed killer, harm other living creatures, including humans. After examining hundreds of scientific studies, the World Health Organization concluded that glyphosate was "probably carcinogenic to humans." Bayer, the main producer of glyphosate, has agreed to pay billions of dollars to settle tens of thousands of lawsuits from people who say the weed killer gave them cancer.

GLYPHOSATE

Regenerative Agriculture

When it comes to reducing our carbon footprint, the benefits of some organic food can be marginal. Small-scale organic farms tend to have a lower carbon footprint, but large organic farms often rely on monocultures and tillage, both of which deplete nutrients and release carbon stored in the soil, as well as agricultural machines that burn fossil fuels. Very often, organic food sold by large retailers has traveled hundreds of miles and is packaged in plastic containers and bags that end up in the trash.

If we want to further reduce carbon emissions while protecting the environment, we can buy food from producers that use regenerative farming methods. These farmers have a holistic approach to agriculture that aims to increase soil health, protect animal welfare, and ensure that workers are treated fairly. These methods include:

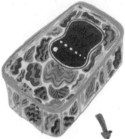

NOT AS SUSTAINABLE AS YOU MIGHT THINK!

Not using agrochemicals or GMOs.

Planting cover crops that fertilize the soil. These include clover, mustard, alfalfa, rye, buckwheat, cowpeas, and radish. These crops are planted in between growing seasons to increase nutrients in the soil and reduce erosion.

Tilling as little as possible. Instead of plowing the field, which disturbs microorganisms and releases carbon, farmers plant directly into the undisturbed soil.

Using crop rotation. When farmers grow different crops from one year to the next, it helps keep soils healthy. For instance, farmers may first grow cereals and then legumes, which have a symbiotic relationship with soil bacteria. These microorganisms extract nitrogen from the air and fix it into the soil, increasing fertility and reducing the need for fertilizers.

Protecting the rights of farm laborers. Farmworkers receive fair payments and benefits, are not forced to work overtime, and are allowed to unionize.

Considering the welfare of animals. In regenerative agriculture, farm animals are treated humanely, are pasture raised or given feed grown using organic methods, and are kept in environments where they are free from discomfort, fear, and distress. They are also given access to the outdoors for long periods of time.

FOOD GROWN USING REGENERATIVE METHODS CAN BE HARD TO IDENTIFY, BUT MANY SMALL ORGANIC FARMERS FOLLOW THESE PRINCIPLES. THE BEST WAY TO KNOW IF THAT'S THE CASE IS TO GET TO KNOW YOUR LOCAL FARMERS BY BUYING FOOD DIRECTLY FROM THEM.

The remarkable thing about soil is that it can be healed. Regenerative agriculture can turn completely dead soil into rich, dark soil, teeming with microorganisms that help sequester carbon.

The Three Sisters

Corn, beans, and squash have been the staple crops of Native American communities for centuries. These plants are known as the Three Sisters because they help each other grow. Corn provides tall stalks for the beans to climb, beans help garner nitrogen from the air to fertilize the soil and prop up the tall corn, and the large squash leaves deprive weeds of sunlight and help retain soil moisture. The crops provide plenty of nutrients for a healthy diet. Corn is rich in carbohydrates, beans have proteins and amino acids, and squash is rich in vitamins and minerals.

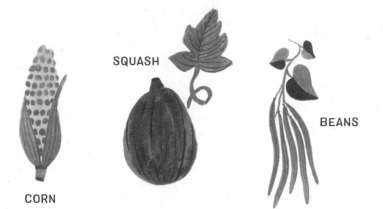

SQUASH

BEANS

CORN

THE FIRST GROUP TO CALL THESE CROPS THE THREE SISTERS WERE THE HAUDENOSAUNEE, ALSO KNOWN AS THE IROQUOIS. THEIR PLANTING METHOD CALLS FOR THE THREE SISTERS TO BE PLANTED TOGETHER, ON THE SAME MOUND.

Urban Farms

Cities can play a key role in transforming the food system. Urban dwellers have become alienated from rural areas, where most of the food is produced. Bringing farming to or around urban areas would allow people to reconnect with food. Urban farming also makes sense because, by 2050, 80 percent of food will be consumed by people living in cities.

Urban farms tend to be more eco-friendly because they don't need to transport their products over long distances—that means less fuel for transportation, less packaging, and less food waste because products often reach customers only hours after being harvested.

Urban farming can ameliorate environmental problems by increasing vegetation cover, removing atmospheric carbon dioxide, and offering a habitat for bees and other pollinators. Urban farming can actually cool urban areas by reducing the heat island effect, which occurs when cities get warmer than nearby rural areas due to heat trapped by asphalt and concrete.

Innovation is the driving force of urban farming. Since space and water are limited, urban farms are forced to adopt cutting-edge technology to be highly efficient. Tools such as artificial intelligence, LED grow lights, robotics, and automated irrigation systems are often used to optimize production. By establishing synergies with other businesses, many of these farms are able to radically reduce the waste they create. And food waste is abundant in cities, which can provide farms with plenty of organic fertilizer to grow crops. For instance, Rotterdam's RotterZwam uses coffee grounds to grow oyster mushrooms.

Urban farms alone cannot transform the food system, but they can be a catalyst for positive change. It is already happening—urban farming is flourishing from New York to Montreal and from Paris to Shanghai, offering millions of people a more environmentally friendly way to eat.

Things You Can Do
to further reduce the carbon impact of your diet

Buy local products. They are fresher and taste better, and the farther away a product was made, the more carbon was used to ship it to you. If you live in North America or Europe, chances are the avocados, bananas, coffee, and cocoa that you buy are produced thousands of miles away. Perishable items like tropical fruits (including pineapples and mangos), asparagus, green beans, and berries are sometimes transported by air.

Avoid buying food in supermarkets. Meat monopolies and industrial farms rely on supermarkets to sell their products. Most processed food products sold in large grocery stores contain synthetic food additives, such as colorants and preservatives, some of which are derived from fossil fuels.

Join a CSA. Community-supported agriculture is a system in which consumers commit to buying a share of a farm's harvest and receive regular deliveries of food products directly from farmers. It is the best option for those who want to get to know their farmers. CSA farmers often have open days in which members can visit their farms and learn how their food is produced.

Buy in season. Local seasonal crops have more flavor because they are picked at their peak of ripeness. They have a smaller carbon footprint because they don't have to be transported over long distances and less energy is required to store them. Out-of-season produce is not as flavorful because it has to be harvested before it ripens.

NEW YORK
Summer

CALIFORNIA
Winter

Eat fresh. Frozen food typically has a larger carbon footprint than fresh food because it needs to be refrigerated, which requires energy. That doesn't mean you should avoid frozen food altogether, only that it is preferable to choose fresh products, if possible.

Cook at home. Be it a carrot soup or a Sunday roast, cooking your own food instead of buying prepared meals or ordering takeout is empowering because it allows you to select ingredients that are sustainably produced. By cooking food at home, you will be able to reduce the emissions associated with large-scale food manufacturing and packaging.

Grow your own food. Sprouts, microgreens (such as beets, radishes, kale, Swiss chard, and basil), scallions, lettuce, and hot peppers are good indoor options. If you have a garden or a balcony with plenty of sunlight, tomatoes, eggplants, and peppers are pretty easy to grow. Some good winter crops are carrots and potatoes. The options are infinite.

BEAR IN MIND THAT BY AND LARGE, MOST OF THE CARBON EMISSIONS LINKED TO FOOD COME FROM FARMING, BUT TRANSPORTATION, PROCESSING, PACKAGING, AND RETAIL ARE LINKED TO ADDITIONAL EMISSIONS.

Rob Greenfield

Adventurer, environmental activist, humanitarian, and "dude making a difference"

When I was younger, I led a consumerist lifestyle. But in 2011, when I was about twenty-five years old, I started to realize that almost everything that I was doing was causing destruction to the Earth. The food I was eating, the car I was driving, the gas I was pumping into the car, the stuff I was buying, the trash I was creating—all of that was causing destruction. That's when I decided to radically transform my life.

Over the course of the next decade, I adopted hundreds of small changes, every single one of them was good for myself and good for the planet, which inspired me to make more changes.

I also took on extreme endeavors to get people to self-reflect, think critically, and ask questions.

I dove into about two thousand dumpsters to show how much food is wasted in the U.S., lived in a fifty-square-foot tiny home drinking rainwater and relying solely on the electricity produced by a small off-grid solar unit, and became the Trash Man, walking around New York City with all the trash I was creating strapped to my body for a month.

I realized that the food I was eating was causing destruction, so I wanted to see if it would be possible to step away from the industrial food system by growing and foraging a hundred percent of my food for a year.

I moved to Orlando, Florida, where I met people in the neighborhood and turned their lawns into gardens and grew over a hundred foods in them—sweet potatoes, yucca, carrots, beans, peppers. I harvested over two hundred species of vegetables and fruits from nature, raised my own bees, and collected salt from seawater. I ended up eating the healthiest of my entire life.

"We can design our lives to be of service to humanity and Earth, while at the same time improving our quality of life both mentally and physically."

Things You Can Do
to reduce food waste

Familiarize yourself with food labels. A product that is past its "best before" date by a short period of time is probably safe to eat.

Avoid impulsive shopping. Plan your meals for the week before you head to the grocery store. That way you will only buy what you need.

Go small. When ordering food from a restaurant or being served at a social gathering, go for a small portion.

Pick ugly fruits and vegetables. One-third of all fruit and vegetables don't make it to plates because they are not attractive enough, but they taste just as good as their Instagram-perfect alternatives! *

* "Everything has beauty, but not everyone sees it."

—Confucius

Love your leftovers. You can have them for lunch the following day or freeze them for the future.

Share. If you throw a dinner party, ask your guests to take leftovers with them. You can also donate extra food to food banks, shelters, and soup kitchens.

FIRST IN FIRST OUT

Practice "first in, first out." Take a look at your fridge and pantry every now and then and put the products that are close to expiring at the front to ensure that you eat them first.

Preserve your food. You can pickle all kinds of foods by submerging them in brine or vinegar: carrots, onions, eggs, herring, olives—the choices are endless. Jams, marmalades, and jellies are a great way to preserve fruit before it goes bad. You can try submerging food items like cheese or tuna in olive oil to preserve them for days, even weeks.

Compost Your Organic Waste

Food scraps and yard waste make up about a third of a household's total waste. These materials release methane when they end up in the landfill. When you compost them, however, you basically feed them to bacteria, protozoa, and fungi. In turn, these tiny creatures convert organic waste into fertilizer. Compost improves soil fertility and allows it to capture more carbon from the atmosphere.

Drop off your food scraps at a local composting bin. Some community gardens have composting bins, as do some food co-ops and farmers markets. If your neighborhood has a curbside compost program, make sure you follow the waste company's guidelines.

Before composting food scraps, clean up all plastic elements, such as elastic bands, twist ties, and stickers.

You can compost all kinds of food waste, but meat, fish, and dairy products are better avoided because they may create smells and attract rodents.

You can also try composting at home.

You can use worms for indoor composting. There are thousands of species of earthworms but only seven that eat food scraps. *Eisenia fetida* worms, also known as red wigglers, are commonly used for vermicomposting. They eat about 25 percent of their body weight each day. So if you start with 1 pound of worms, you need to feed your bin ¼ pound of food scraps every day. Vermicomposting has its limitations—worms don't like garlic, onion scraps, or citrus fruits.

If you have a backyard, you can try building a compost bin.

The ideal ratio is to mix one part of green materials (food scraps, coffee grounds, tea bags, etc.) with two parts of brown materials (leaves, shredded newspaper, twigs, wood shavings, sawdust, etc.).

Chopping the food waste into smaller parts will speed up the process.

You will need to remix, or aerate, the contents of the bin at least once a week so that the microbes decomposing the scraps can breathe.

The moisture content should be between 50 and 60 percent. Most of the moisture will come from the food scraps themselves, but you may need to add some water.

For the first few days the pile should reach a temperature between 50° and 110°F, which will increase to 130° to 160°F over the first couple of weeks. From then on, temperatures should drop to between 50° and 100°F again.

AFTER 8 TO 12 WEEKS, THE COMPOST SHOULD BE DARK AND CRUMBLY. THAT MEANS IT IS READY TO BE USED! YOU CAN MIX IT WITH THE SOIL IN YOUR GARDEN TO HELP PLANTS GROW STRONG AND HEALTHY. COMPOSTING IS ALSO GOOD FOR THE CLIMATE BECAUSE HEALTHIER PLANTS ABSORB MORE CARBON FROM THE ATMOSPHERE.

Things You Can Do
to ensure that your barbecue is climate-friendly

Choose the right grill. Charcoal grills typically generate three times more greenhouse emissions than gas grills. Electric grills are also a valid option—but given that fossil fuels, especially coal, are often burned to produce power, in most cases a gas grill is still the most sustainable choice.

Planning ahead and avoiding impulsive purchases will allow you to avoid food waste.

Serve food and drinks in reusable plates and cups. Avoid single-use knives and forks.

Use less meat. Blend veggies or mushrooms with ground meat to create a more sustainable burger.

Choose free-range, organic turkey or chicken over beef.

Experiment with plant-based patties. These create less greenhouse gas emissions and require less water and land than beef burger patties.

Grill up a heap of vegetables. Grilled peppers, onions, and eggplant taste great with a tangy sauce.

_ _ _

FOUR

Eco Travel

Cars, buses, trains, planes, motorbikes, boats . . . most means of transport are powered by oil, and oil means carbon emissions and deadly pollution that taints the air we breathe. Cars are by far the biggest culprit, and the problem is getting worse because people are increasingly choosing to drive bigger, more powerful cars that spit more carbon dioxide into the atmosphere. But there are environmentally friendly options to move around. Public transportation is growing in many cities. Walking and biking produce no emissions and provide us with a direct connection to the environment. And electric vehicles and e-scooters are quickly becoming mainstream.

Motorized Transport = Greenhouse Gases

Worldwide, the transportation sector is responsible for about 15 percent of total greenhouse gas emissions.

The sources of those emissions include:

 Road transport. This includes emissions from cars, trucks, lorries, motorcycles, and buses. Passenger cars alone consume about a quarter of all the oil produced worldwide.

 Aviation. Most emissions from aviation come from passenger travel, but the transportation of goods by plane also creates emissions.

Shipping. Passenger and cargo ships that transport goods around the world emit greenhouse gases.

 Rail. Passenger and freight trains add to carbon emissions.

Pipelines. Fossil fuels are often transported via pipelines. This requires energy inputs, which results in emissions.

TRANSPORTATION EMISSIONS BY INDUSTRY

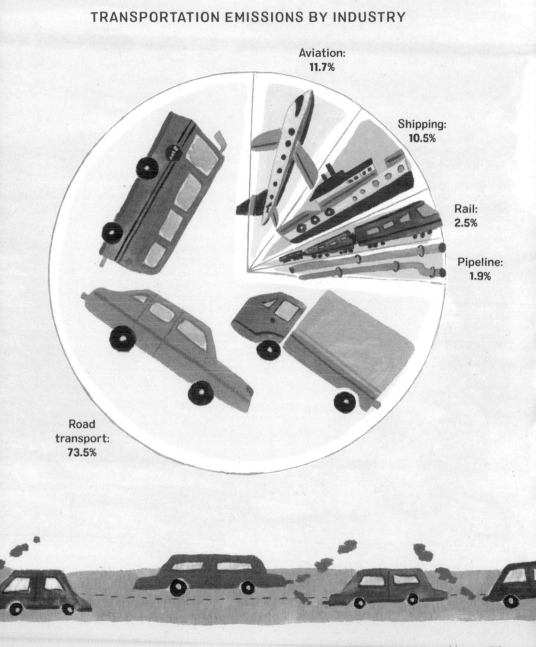

Aviation:
11.7%

Shipping:
10.5%

Rail:
2.5%

Pipeline:
1.9%

Road
transport:
73.5%

A Brief History of the Car

Cars have been around for a little over a century. The father of modern cars was a German engineer named Karl Benz, who in 1886 patented the Motorwagen, a vehicle that looked a lot like a horseless carriage. The Motorwagen featured an internal engine that burned gasoline to produce thrust. Three years later, his wife, Bertha Benz, took their teenage sons on a 66-mile-long trip to demonstrate that the vehicle was safe to drive. The first-ever road trip received a lot of publicity, generating widespread interest in the Motorwagen.

The Motorwagen was the first of a handful of early motor vehicles that created excitement but failed to become main-stream because they were expensive and unreliable. In 1908, the Ford Motor Company launched the Model T. The car was sturdy and cheap—so much so that it rapidly replaced horses and buggies in the U.S., becoming the first-ever mass-produced motor vehicle. It was also the first car to be assembled in several countries, including Germany, Mexico, and Japan. By 1927, Ford had produced 15 million Model Ts.

After the Model T, cars quickly became mainstream all over the world. Hundreds of different models have been launched, with some having sold tens of millions of units.

Volkswagen Beetle (1938–2019), 24 million units. The Beetle was commissioned by Adolf Hitler, who wanted to create a car for the masses. Despite its dark origins, the Love Bug became the car of the hippies in the 1960s and was hugely popular in faraway markets such as Mexico, Brazil, and South Africa.

Toyota Corolla (1966–present), 44 million units. The Corolla lacks bells and whistles but has the landmarks of a best-selling car—it is practical, reliable, and affordable. If all the Toyota Corollas that have been sold over the years were placed next to one another, the line would be long enough to go around the world five times.

Lada Classic (1970–2015), 19 million units. First produced by AvtoVAZ of Russia, the Classic was known for its spartan interiors and reliability. It became an instant success in the Soviet Union, where prospective buyers often had to wait for years to get one. Its low selling price and durability made it popular in many overseas markets, including Canada, the U.K., and New Zealand.

Ford F-150 (1948–present), 40 million units. The most popular car in the U.S. in the second half of the 20th century, the Ford F-150 marked a shift toward pickup trucks and sport utility vehicles (SUVs), which have become mainstream on American roads.

Nowadays, there are at least 1.5 billion motor vehicles worldwide, and a network of around 25 million miles of roads has been built for them—that's about 100 times the distance from Earth to the moon!

The Problem with SUVs

Carbon emissions keep increasing worldwide because we continue relying on fossil fuels to produce power. But it's also because drivers are buying more SUVs. These cars use 25 percent more fuel than medium-sized sedans because they are heavier, have more powerful engines, and are less aerodynamic.

There are now about 200 million SUVs worldwide, up from 35 million in 2010.

Although this shift is happening worldwide, it is being led by the U.S., where smaller cars that get more miles to the gallon have been going out of fashion for years. Nowadays, seven of every ten cars sold in the U.S. fall into the "large" category that includes SUVs, pickup trucks, and vans. There are more than 60 million large cars on US roads, and they are the main reason why the country's transportation system emits more greenhouse gases than the entire economies of France and the U.K. combined.

Why have SUVs conquered the world? The reason is twofold. On the one hand, carmakers are launching more SUVs because they make more money selling bigger cars. On the other, drivers want larger and more powerful vehicles because cars are the ultimate status symbol.

The average US passenger car has 200 horsepower and weighs 1.6 metric tons, compared to 125 horsepower and 1.4 metric tons for vehicles in the European Union.

SHARE OF SUVS IN TOTAL CAR SALES*

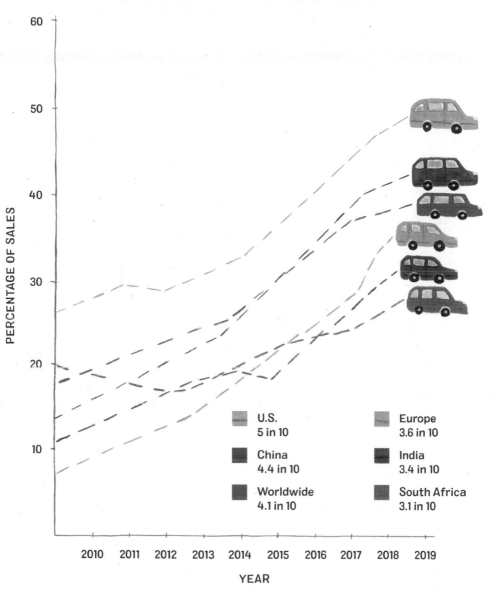

PERCENTAGE OF SALES

60

50

40

30

20

10

2010 2011 2012 2013 2014 2015 2016 2017 2018 2019

YEAR

U.S.
5 in 10

China
4.4 in 10

Worldwide
4.1 in 10

Europe
3.6 in 10

India
3.4 in 10

South Africa
3.1 in 10

*New car sales

Smog

Carbon dioxide is only part of the story. Cars, trucks, and motorbikes that burn fossil fuels also emit toxic gases and particles such as:

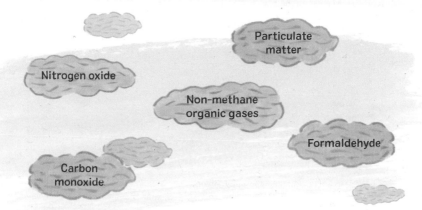

These gases and tiny particles stay close to the ground. In large cities, they often form smog, a brown haze that pollutes the air and is toxic to humans. The term *smog* was first used in the early 20th century to describe the combination of smoke and fog in London.

Each year, smog contributes to millions of early deaths from stroke, heart disease, lung cancer, and respiratory ailments. Some of these particles can react with sunlight to produce ozone, a gas that can trigger a wide array of health problems, including chest pain, coughing, and throat irritation. And new research shows that air pollution impairs cognitive function, especially among children and the elderly.

Walking and Biking

The best solution is often the simplest. Half of all car trips are less than 3 miles long. That means that we often take the car when walking or biking will do just fine!

Public Transportation

Buses, trains, subways, streetcars, trolleys, tramways, monorails, cable cars, ferries . . . public transportation takes many shapes and forms. When it comes to reducing the carbon footprint of transportation, sharing is caring. A bus full of passengers can take more than 40 cars off the road, while subways and trains can transport hundreds of passengers at a time.

But not everybody has access to public transportation. On average, 80 percent of Europeans have easy access to subways, commuter trains, and bus routes because their governments have invested heavily to build them. Whereas Paris, Madrid, and London have substantially extended their subway and rail systems in recent years, only 26 miles of subways and elevated trains were built in the U.S. between 2010 and 2019. That's why only 55 percent of Americans have access to public transportation.

Going to School

Biking, walking, skateboarding, and rollerblading are the most environmentally friendly ways to go to school because they produce zero emissions. On top of that, these so-called active school transport options help us stay healthy, reducing obesity rates among kids and parents.

Electric bikes designed to transport up to three small children are becoming increasingly popular. They come in many shapes and forms. Some of them have boxes in the front or back to transport passengers, whereas others have additional seats.

For those who live farther away, the school bus is a great option. A school bus can replace dozens of cars on the roads, which obviously means less carbon dioxide but also less traffic-related air pollution, less noise, and less congestion. In the U.S., some 26 million children take the school bus every day, which means millions fewer cars on the roads. And school buses save hundreds of lives each year because students are 70 times more likely to get to school safely if they travel by bus instead of by car.

Things You Can Do
to improve your fuel efficiency and slash your car's emissions

Make sure that your tires are inflated to the recommended pressure. Check their pressure every few months and right before starting a road trip.

Don't keep unnecessary stuff in the trunk. For every 100 pounds of weight, your vehicle's energy efficiency decreases by 1 to 2 percent.

Buy a set of low rolling resistance tires. These tires generate less friction when they roll on the road, increasing your vehicle's fuel efficiency.

Keep your car tuned up. Follow your carmaker's manual to find out when it is time for maintenance. Simple things like regular oil changes, air-filter changes, and spark plug replacements can boost fuel efficiency.

Maintain a cruise speed. Once you hit the highway, try to drive at a speed of 55 to 60 miles per hour and maintain a constant speed. Driving at a fast speed will increase aerodynamic drag, forcing your car to burn more fuel. You can also use cruise control—it saves gas!

Drive smoothly. Speeding, rapid acceleration, and abrupt braking can lower your gas mileage by up to 40 percent in stop-and-go traffic.

Avoid idling. Shut down your engine when you're not moving—in parking lots, when you're waiting for someone, or when unloading your car. In the U.S., eliminating the idling of personal vehicles would be the same as taking 5 million vehicles off the road.

Use your AC moderately. If it is not too hot, opening your windows instead of turning on the AC will often be enough if you're driving at a moderate speed. The AC may be the most efficient way to cool your car when you drive at a high speed because lowering your windows will increase drag, which in turn will increase fuel consumption.

Shared Micromobility

In recent years, a wide array of small electric vehicles has arrived on the roads and sidewalks of major cities. E-bikes, e-scooters, and e-mopeds are ideal for short trips and can be rented for very little money by using a smartphone. Some companies even offer unlimited monthly trips for a small fee, and some public transportation systems include bike-share options in their transit cards. On top of that, users don't have to pay for repairs or worry about maintenance.

Shared micromobility means that individuals don't need to rely on cars for all their transportation needs. Research shows that people are increasingly using these battery-powered vehicles to go shopping, run errands, and commute to work. And, best of all, some are using them instead of cars!

In addition to helping slash emissions from the transportation sector, small electric vehicles can help reduce noise and congestion in urban areas and have a much smaller environmental footprint than cars because they don't need as many resources to be built. However, some of the electricity that powers these vehicles is generated by burning fossil fuels, so walking or riding a regular bicycle will always be better for the environment.

FIND YOUR VEHICLE

DOWNLOAD THE APP

DON'T FORGET YOUR HELMET!

Electric Vehicles (EVs)

A decade ago, EVs were a novelty for tech-savvy eccentrics, but things have changed. There are now dozens of models out there, from low-cost utility cars to superfast convertibles and everything in between. That's *great* news for the environment because EVs have no tailpipe emissions, meaning they don't emit toxic particles that can be harmful when inhaled, like nitrogen oxides and volatile organic compounds.

EVs can indirectly emit carbon dioxide, however, because the energy they use is often generated by burning fossil fuels. Charging an EV in Iceland or Brazil has a very small carbon footprint because those countries produce most of their electricity with renewables. But if you live in Poland or China, the electricity that charges your EV is produced mainly by burning coal, which means that your car is indirectly spitting a lot of carbon dioxide into the atmosphere. But by and large, EVs have a much smaller carbon footprint than traditional cars because the vast majority of countries produce some electricity using renewables.

EVS HAVE OTHER ADVANTAGES, TOO

⚡ National and local governments provide tax credits and subsidies to make EVs more affordable.

⚡ EVs are much cheaper to run per mile traveled because the electricity they use costs less than gasoline.

⚡ They are also less expensive to maintain because their motors don't include parts that often need servicing, such as exhaust systems, starter motors, and fuel injection systems. There are fewer liquids to change, like oil or transmission fluid, and EV brake systems typically last longer than those on conventional vehicles.

⚡ Most drivers will only need to use a charging station when they go on a long road trip because EVs can be charged at home. Most EVs can travel more than 100 miles on a charge, and many of them have a range of more than 300 miles.

⚡ Charging an empty battery can take quite a few hours. But many modern EVs accept fast charging, which allows for loading enough power to ride more than 50 miles in just 20 minutes.

⚡ Cities like Madrid and London have restricted combustion-engine cars from their urban centers to reduce pollution, but EVs are exempt from these restrictions.

⚡ EVs are whisper quiet, which means less noise pollution.

Effective Motors

Another reason why EVs are better for the environment is that they are much more efficient.

Traditional cars are inherently wasteful because about 70 percent of the energy produced by their engines is lost as heat and through engine friction. A small part of the energy is used to power parts of the engine like the water pump, fuel pump, and oil pump. As a result, only about **25 percent** of the energy produced by a car's combustion engine actually reaches its wheels.

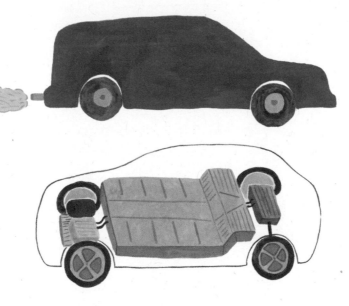

EVs convert about **75 percent** of the electricity they use into thrust, while the rest is lost when it moves through the different components of the drivetrain and when the battery is charged. EVs waste energy by braking, but they use regenerative braking to recoup some of that energy.

Go Small

To ensure that your future electric car has a low carbon footprint, go small. The production of EVs is more carbon-intensive than the manufacturing of combustion engine cars, primarily because they are powered by rechargeable batteries that feature a variety of metals and minerals, including cobalt, lithium, nickel, and manganese, as well as rare earth elements, all of which need to be mined in faraway places, processed, and transported. In addition, battery production requires copious amounts of energy. As well as much bigger batteries, larger EVs feature more steel, aluminum, and plastic. What all this means is that the production of an electric car has a relatively big environmental footprint, and the bigger the car, the bigger the footprint.

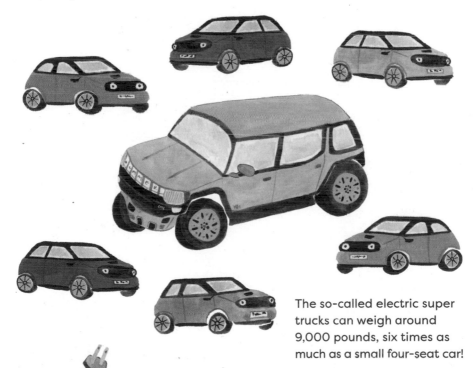

The so-called electric super trucks can weigh around 9,000 pounds, six times as much as a small four-seat car!

Car Sharing

Buying an EV is always a more environmentally friendly option than getting a gasoline-powered car, but not buying a car at all is even better. The reason is simple—we need fewer cars on the road so that we can create more space for less-polluting forms of transportation.

And for those times that you need a car ride, remember that car sharing is associated with fewer emissions than individual car ownership. Sharing vehicles is easy. Here are your options:

Ride-hailing. Getting a ride on Uber or Lyft is linked to high emissions due to deadheading, a term used to describe the miles driven without passengers in the car. Lyft and Uber have said that all the vehicles in their platforms will be electric by 2030 and 2040, respectively. But, until then, the best way to limit the emissions is to share the ride with other passengers by choosing the pooling option.

Carpooling. Carpools typically involve coworkers or students riding together to save on fuel. There are apps that connect drivers who have empty seats with people looking for a ride, such as BlaBlaCar, a French company that now operates in 22 countries, and Via, which allows passengers heading in the same direction to share a ride.

Carshare. Members of a carshare can typically borrow a car owned by a private company and pay per mile, minute, or hour. The most popular car-sharing companies are car2go and Zipcar. Car2go has introduced EVs in several cities, including Paris, Montreal, and Madrid, and Zipcar offers EVs in London.

Peer-to-peer. Through P2P online platforms such as Getaround, car owners can rent their vehicles to other people to make some extra money. Some of these platforms use technology that allows renters to open the cars they borrow using their smartphones.

Things You Can Do
to reduce carbon emissions from online shopping

Order sparingly and buy in volume. One big order, instead of several smaller ones, means fewer trucks on the road churning out carbon dioxide.

Say no to express delivery. Delivery companies need to make more trips when customers choose expedited shipping.

Buy carefully. More returns mean more trucks on the road.

Choose locker delivery. Some online retailers give customers the option of having their packages delivered to a nearby location, which leads to fewer trucks on the road.

Look for zero-emissions deliveries. They are rare, but some start-ups deliver groceries by bike.

Recycle packaging material and buy from sellers that pack their products in paper instead of plastic. Some restaurants deliver food in reusable containers, and some sellers use plastic-free packaging.

The Carbon Footprint of Online Shopping

In just a few years, online shopping has taken over the world. From groceries to electronics, furniture, toys, and clothes, people are increasingly relying on the internet to shop. But ordering online has led to more delivery trucks on the roads—the number in the world's largest 100 cities is expected to increase from 5.3 million in 2019 to 7.2 million in 2030. That means more noise, pollution, and traffic, which is no good for the climate.

If you're ordering online instead of driving to the store, chances are that your carbon footprint has decreased. But if you regularly use public transportation or a bike to go to the store, online shopping will increase your emissions.

Cut Down on Flying

Although flying represents only about 2 percent of our global carbon emissions, airplanes have a huge carbon footprint when compared to other forms of transportation. For instance, a round-trip flight from the U.S. to Europe emits roughly 1 metric ton of carbon dioxide per passenger—equivalent to 20 percent of the average annual emissions for a person living in Spain or Italy. Flying first class results in at least twice the emissions because of how much space is reserved for each passenger.

Air traffic has been growing rapidly for decades. By 2019, airplanes transported 4.3 billion passengers on some 126,000 daily flights. Back then, researchers predicted that emissions from air traveling could triple by 2050. Although air traffic decreased dramatically due to the COVID-19 pandemic, the airline industry is expected to recover, thanks in part to a growing middle class in Asia, where many of the fastest growing airports are located.

If you have no choice but to take a plane, the International Council on Clean Transportation recommends flying like a **NERD**:

Newer planes, like the Airbus A320neo or Boeing 787-8, are more energy-efficient.

Economy seats typically result in fewer emissions per passenger.

Regular midsized jets tend to be more energy-efficient than large ones.

Direct flights produce less emissions than those with layovers.

Mara Rosén

No-fly pioneer and founding member of We Stay on the Ground and Flight Free World

I gave up flying in 2008 because I became aware of how serious the climate crisis is. A lot of climate-aware people eat less meat, avoid plastic bags, and cycle to work, but the moment they get on a long-haul flight, they cancel out all the good things they do to reduce emissions.

That's why in 2017 I started a campaign to encourage people to give up flying for a year. For the first campaign, which was called Flight Free 2019, we received about ten thousand pledges, mostly from Sweden. That year, flying in Sweden decreased by four percent. That may not sound like a lot, but you have to understand that before then, flying had been increasing steadily every year.

In 2020, we received about twenty-six thousand no-fly pledges from people in thirty-two countries. The term *flygskam,* which translates as "flight shame," has become popular all over the world, prompting the International Air Transport Association to say that the no-fly movement presents a threat to the industry.

What I learned from our campaigns is that if you do the right thing and talk about it, others will follow, and that will pave the way for the systemic change we need.

"People are underestimating their ability to change the world."

- - -

FIVE

What a Waste

To make the things we buy every day, companies extract natural resources from the planet that can't be put back. Factories emit greenhouse gases when they turn those resources into electronics, domestic appliances, furniture, clothes, toiletries, kitchen utensils—you name it. After we use these products, we discard them, sometimes within seconds, creating swaths of waste and pollution that taint the air we breathe, the water we drink, and the land we live on. To cut our carbon footprints, we need to waste less, say no to disposable plastic, recycle effectively, use what we have, and think twice before we buy.

The World Has a Waste Problem

People are trashy. Those of us living in developed countries generate between 2 and 5 pounds of trash per day.

TRASH GENERATION RATES (POUNDS/PERSON/DAY):

4.9 lbs   4.3 lbs   3.8 lbs   3.4 lbs

2.9 lbs   2.7 lbs   0.9 lb   1.6 lbs

When compared to those living in large, developed countries, the average American wins the trash competition by generating nearly ten times their body weight in trash every year. Throughout their lifetimes, Americans send around 64 metric tons of waste to the landfill.

Household Trash

THIS IS WHAT HOUSEHOLD TRASH TYPICALLY INCLUDES:

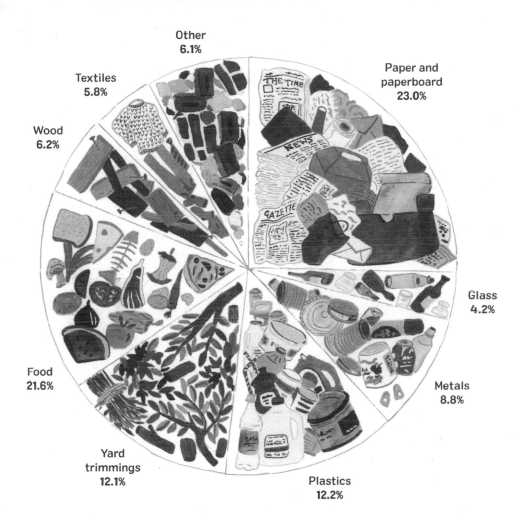

Other
6.1%

Textiles
5.8%

Wood
6.2%

Paper and
paperboard
23.0%

Glass
4.2%

Metals
8.8%

Food
21.6%

Yard
trimmings
12.1%

Plastics
12.2%

Most of Our Trash Doesn't Get a Second Chance

| United States **50%** | United States **23.6%** |
| European Union **24%** | European Union **31%** |

LANDFILL

Half of US trash ends up in a landfill, where much of it decomposes and emits methane, a powerful greenhouse gas.

RECYCLING

About a quarter of US trash gets recycled into new products.

United States **11.8%**
European Union **27%**

United States **14.6%**
European Union **18%**

INCINERATION

A good portion of US trash is burned. Power plants that burn trash to generate energy release air pollutants (carbon dioxide, heavy metals, dioxins, and particulate matter) that contribute to climate change and are toxic to humans.

COMPOSTING

A growing portion of US trash is composted. When we compost food waste and yard trimmings, we basically feed them to bacteria, protozoa, and fungi. In turn, these tiny creatures convert organic waste into fertilizer to help plants grow.

The Plastic Problem

Plastics have a very large environmental footprint. They are not biodegradable and are very difficult to recycle— in large part because they feature in countless products of all shapes and sizes.

PLASTICS belong to a category of materials called polymers—a word that comes from two Greek words: *poly*, meaning "many," and *meros*, meaning "parts" or "units." Synthetic polymers are produced using carbon atoms in fossil fuels and hydrogen, but they may also contain oxygen, chlorine, fluorine, nitrogen, silicon, phosphorus, and sulfur.

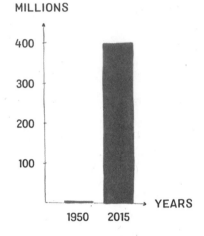

MILLIONS

400

300

200

100

YEARS

1950   2015

The **first synthetic polymer** was invented by Leo Hendrik Baekeland in 1907. The product was called Bakelite, and the polymer is poly-oxybenzylmethylenglycolanhydride, with the formula $(C_6H_6O \cdot CH_2O)_n$. Bakelite was a huge success. By 1944, when Baekeland died, his invention featured in more than 15,000 different products, including jewelry, cameras, and early machine guns. By then, the global production of Bakelite was around 160,000 metric tons.

Plastic production took off during World War II. Nylon replaced silk in the manufacturing of parachutes, synthetic rubber was used to produce tires, and Plexiglas was used to make submarine periscopes, aircraft windshields, and gun turrets.

Global production of plastics increased from 2 million metric tons in 1950 to around 380 million metric tons in 2015.

Bakelite $(C_6H_6O \cdot CH_2O)_n$
The chemical name of
Bakelite is

polyoxybenzylmethylenglycolanhydride

Nowadays, plastics are everywhere we look. But they are also hidden from view.

Plastics are widely used in construction for insulation, pipes, windows, and roofs.

More clothing is made out of polyester and nylon—both plastics—than cotton and wool.

Plastics account for up to 50 percent of a vehicle's volume.

The Carbon Footprint of Plastic

Most of the 8.3 billion metric tons (MT) of plastics produced since 1950 still exist in the environment, in one form or another.

Approximately **2.5 billion metric tons** (about **30%** of all plastics ever produced) are still in use.

8.3 BILLION
METRIC TONS

Approximately **5.8 billion metric tons** have been discarded. The vast majority of this wasted plastic is either in landfills or the environment.

Just **600 million metric tons** have been recycled.*

Includes plastics that have been recycled more than once.

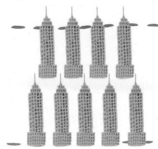

If current trends continue, by 2050 there will be roughly **12 billion metric tons** of plastic waste in landfills or the natural environment. That's 35,000 times as heavy as the Empire State Building!

Because they are made with fossil fuels, plastics are linked to high carbon emissions. Between now and 2050, emissions from producing and incinerating plastics could amount to 56 billion metric tons of carbon—almost 50 times the annual emissions of all of the coal power plants in the U.S. Unless we drastically reduce plastic production, we won't be able to slow down climate change.

But the problem is only getting worse. Since 2010, the petrochemical industry has invested nearly $97 billion in approximately 230 projects to expand operations along the Gulf Coast, which is home to Dow Chemical's Freeport, Texas, plant—the largest petrochemical facility in the western hemisphere. An additional 120 projects are under construction or in the planning phase.

The industry wants to take advantage of the so-called shale gas revolution. In 2019, the United States produced 34 trillion cubic feet of natural gas, almost twice as much as in 2005. Most of the new gas comes from deposits trapped under fine-grained sedimentary rocks known as shale. Shale gas is plentiful and inexpensive to extract.

SHALE GAS CONTAINS ETHANE, WHICH CAN BE CONVERTED TO ETHYLENE—THE SOURCE OF ABOUT TWO-THIRDS OF THE WORLD'S PLASTIC PRODUCTION.

The United States is now the top ethane exporter, sending it to petrochemical plants in Canada, Brazil, India, Europe, and China.

TOP US NATURAL GAS PRODUCERS

1. Texas
2. Pennsylvania
3. Louisiana
4. Oklahoma
5. Ohio

Plastic in Nature

Plastics also pollute the environment.

An estimated **11 million metric tons** of plastic enters our oceans every year, where it tends to break down into smaller parts and is ingested by wildlife. Experts estimate that by 2050, the total amount of plastic waste in the oceans will weigh more than all marine fish.

Ocean currents push plastic debris toward five garbage patches. The largest of them is the Great Pacific Garbage Patch, located halfway between Hawaii and California and covering an area three times the size of France.

These four brands are responsible for more than half a million metric tons of plastic pollution in China, India, the Philippines, Brazil, Mexico, and Nigeria every year. That plastic waste is either burned or ends up in landfills or the environment. Researchers estimate that developing countries account for **50 to 70 percent of the plastic that enters the oceans every year.**

Plastics in Wildlife

Scientists estimate that the amount of plastic entering the oceans might triple by 2040, which is seriously bad news for the ocean and the creatures that live there.

Reports indicate that more than 700 species of marine animals have eaten or been entangled in plastic.

Plastics sometimes can contain chemical additives such as flame retardants and colorants, as well as PFAs, which make some plastics resistant to water, stains, and heat. When ingested, these plastics can transfer these toxins into an organism's bloodstream or tissues.

Researchers often find dead birds with plastic waste in their stomachs. They estimate that by 2050, 99 percent of all seabird species will have ingested plastic waste during their lifetimes.

When they visited Cocos (Keeling) Islands—known as "Australia's last unspoiled paradise"—scientists found 414 million pieces of plastic, including 977,000 shoes and 373,000 toothbrushes.

A whale was found on a Scottish beach in 2019 with 220 pounds of waste in her stomach, including bundles of rope, plastic cups, bags, gloves, and tubing.

An estimated 52 percent of the world's turtles have eaten plastic waste. Galapagos green turtles sometimes get entangled in plastic bags because they look a lot like one of their favorite meals: jellyfish.

Plastics don't biodegrade because they cannot be broken down by microbes. However, after years and years, plastic waste often breaks down into smaller pieces called microplastics, which are often thinner than a human hair. Microplastics can also come from synthetic fibers in clothing and carpets, as well as car tires.

Microplastics are so tiny that they float in the air and can be transported thousands of miles by atmospheric currents.

Researchers have found microplastics in the snow in the Arctic.

Tiny plastic fibers have been detected in otherwise pristine locations like the Rocky Mountains, the Swiss Alps, and the Pyrenees.

Microplastics have been found in 128 brands of commercial salt from 38 different countries spanning over five continents.

Plastics are in our bodies, too. Scientists estimate that the average person ingests or inhales between 74,000 and 121,000 particles of plastic each year. And that number is much higher for those who predominantly drink water from plastic bottles.

The Packaging of Stuff

Every year, 42 percent of all the plastic produced is used to manufacture packaging.

Just because packaging has a recycling code on it does not mean it will be accepted at your local collection site. While ordinances vary across the world, here are some guidelines.

Plastics coded as #1, #2, and #5 are widely accepted throughout the world. Most facilities do not accept plastics coded as #4, #6, and #7, and #3 is definitely a no-no.

- -

1 **polyethylene terephthalate (PET):** soft drink and water bottles

2 **high-density polyethylene (HDPE):** milk containers, squeeze bottles

3 **polyvinyl chloride (PVC):** bottles for some shampoos and cleaning products

4 **low-density polyethylene (LDPE):** plastic bags, some plastic wraps, beverage cups

5 **polypropylene (PP):** yogurt and butter tubs, take-away food containers, ketchup bottles

6 **polystyrene (PS; popularly known as Styrofoam):** beverage/foam cups, toys, the little windows in envelopes, knives and forks, trays for meats, fish, and cheeses

7 **mixed plastic:** items made from different types of plastic or those made with resins that are not recyclable

In the U.S., waste management services collect 35.7 million US tons (that's 218 pounds per person) of plastics every year, and only 9 percent of that is recycled. For comparison, about 40 percent of the 73 pounds of plastic packaging discarded by the average EU citizen gets recycled.

Things You Can Do
to get to zero plastic

Say No to Single-Use Plastic

Eliminating plastic waste will help us protect wildlife and shrink our carbon footprint.

Replace plastic bottles and disposable bags with reusable alternatives.

VS

Shop brands that sell their products in plastic-free packaging.

Bring reusable bags and shop in bulk. Products from the bulk aisle = no packaging! In the long term, buying larger items instead of many small ones will lead to less plastic waste.

Say no to straws, stirrers, and disposable cutlery.

Ask your local coffee shop to pour your coffee in a reusable coffee cup.

Choose aluminum over plastic when you can (it has very high recycling rates), but glass containers are also a good choice.

Avoid items sold in soft plastic packaging. Soft plastics, like food pouches, cling film, and Bubble Wrap are not recyclable.

Avoid PVC. It's not widely used to package food, but some clamshells are made of PVC, as are blister packages. It's not recyclable.

Use your own containers. Many specialty stores and farmers markets sell food with little or no packaging and often agree to place your food in your own containers or in paper bags.

Toward a Zero-Waste Kitchen

Even though disposable plastics seem ubiquitous, there are many Things You Can Do to avoid them.

Plan ahead. Impulsive shopping is plastic packaging's best friend. Before you go to the store, look at your calendar, make a menu plan, and write a list of what you actually need.

Use biodegradable products. Buy biodegradable scrubbers, sponges, and brushes to wash your dishes instead of ones made with plastic. Biodegradable dishwashing soap bars are a climate-friendly alternative to the traditional dishwashing liquids that come in plastic bottles and often contain petrochemicals.

Choose utensils that are not plastic. Search for spatulas made of bamboo and stainless steel silverware, which will last a lifetime. Get a wooden chopping board instead of a plastic one. If you treat it with care, it will last many years.

Choose metal or glass containers over plastic alternatives. Stainless steel containers look great and will keep going for years and years.

Broaden your horizons. Plastic packaging is hard to avoid in supermarkets. Fishmongers, butchers, bakeries, and other specialty stores will be happy to wrap your food in wax paper or place it in a reusable container for you.

Avoid plastic food wrap. Keep your food in reusable containers instead. Beeswax food wrap is a great alternative because it is reusable, moldable, and free of petrochemicals. Also, check out reusable silicone lids.

Get some mason jars. If you want to reduce plastic waste in the kitchen, mason jars will be your biggest ally. They come in lots of sizes and can last a lifetime. They are a great way to store staples from the bulk aisle, such as rice and pasta, and to keep food leftovers in the fridge or freezer.

Buy recycled products. We should support the companies that turn our waste into new products. Some brands sell food containers, scrubbers, and insulated bags made with recycled materials.

Lauren Singer

Founder of the Package Free Shop and zero-waste personality who shot to fame thanks to her blog *Trash Is for Tossers*

While studying environmental science, I learned about every terrible thing happening on the planet and how it's impacting not just the birds and the bees and the flowers but also people. Learning about how unsustainably we live made me angry and frustrated. I blamed big businesses. I blamed the government for the lack of policies and regulations. I got super angry. I joined the anti-fracking movement and went to protests. Around that time, I realized there's a huge difference between proselytizing about sustainability and actually living sustainably. I started assessing my life and realized that all my beauty and cleaning products were packaged in plastic and contained synthetic ingredients. The same for all of my clothing. I was protesting against the oil and gas industry, but I was subsidizing them through my consumption habits. There was a massive misalignment between my values and my actions. That motivated me to start cutting plastic out of my life. In 2012, I started buying my groceries without plastic packaging, making my own beauty products, composting, and going to farmers markets. I began collecting the trash that I couldn't avoid in a mason jar and I started my blog *Trash Is for Tossers*. It was empowering because I could, for the first time in my life, have direct control over the impact I was having on the environment. And it resulted in a better lifestyle because I was saving money, not exposing myself to toxic chemicals, and eating significantly better. I also started making my own organic laundry detergent. That's how my first company, Simply Co., was born. I later met entrepreneurs who had launched sustainable products and found out that they were struggling to grow their businesses because they didn't have a direct customer base. The one thing I have, thanks to *Trash Is for Tossers*, is a following of ideal customers. In 2017, I brought these brands under one roof by creating the Package Free Shop. We started with about forty brands and now we have more than one hundred brands, selling almost a thousand products to help make the world less trashy.

"The state of the world is made up of billions of collective actions. If we can evolve ourselves as individuals to make small actions that have a positive impact, ultimately those actions will elevate our overall positive impact on the planet."

The Usual Suspects

In addition to plastic, most of the packaging we use is made of paper, glass, aluminum, and tin.

PAPER

Paper and cardboard are the largest components of household waste, representing about a quarter of all the waste that homes generate. Paper packaging is preferable to a plastic alternative because it has very high recycling rates. However, not all paper products can be recycled. Napkins are usually too soiled to be recycled, and toilet paper ends up down the drain.

IN THE U.S., TWO-THIRDS OF THE 67 MILLION US TONS OF PAPER PRODUCTS DISCARDED IN 2017 WERE RECYCLED. EU PAPER AND CARDBOARD RECYCLING RATES ARE SLIGHTLY HIGHER.

GLASS

Glass packaging is typically used for soft drinks, beer, wine, and liquor bottles, as well as food jars and containers for cosmetics. In some places, clear glass bottles have a higher recycling rate because they are more widely used, but tinted glass bottles get recycled, too. In the U.S., glass recycling reduced greenhouse gas emissions by more than 800,000 million US tons in 2019—equivalent to taking 90,000 cars off the road for a year.

US HOUSEHOLDS RECYCLE ONLY ABOUT 25 PERCENT OF THEIR GLASS; EUROPEAN HOUSEHOLDS RECYCLE 75 PERCENT.

ALUMINUM

Aluminum packaging is used for soft drink and aerosol cans. Aluminum can easily be recycled back into the same product, whereas glass and plastics are often "downcycled" into products of lesser quality, like fiberglass or carpet fibers. Recycling aluminum requires 92 percent less energy than making it from scratch.

ABOUT 50 PERCENT OF ALL THE ALUMINUM CANS GET RECYCLED IN THE U.S. VERSUS 75 PERCENT IN EUROPE.

TIN

Tin cans are made mostly of steel, but they are called tin cans because they are coated with a thin layer of tin to protect the contents' flavor and prevent the can from corroding. Aerosol cans are typically made of steel or aluminum and are also recyclable—just make sure they are empty before you place them in the recycling bin.

ABOUT 75 PERCENT OF ALL THE TIN CANS IN THE U.S. AND EUROPE GET RECYCLED.

Things You Can Do
to ensure that your recyclables get recycled

Sort your plastics. Only hard plastics can be recycled. Soft plastics often get entangled in the machines that separate recyclable items. That's why plastic bags (including grocery bags, Ziploc bags, bread bags, and newspaper bags), food pouches, Bubble Wrap, and inflatables should not go into the recycling bin.

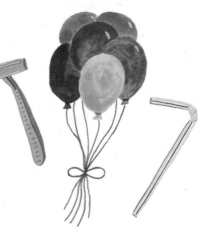

Throw away small plastic and mixed-material objects. Small objects such as plastic utensils and straws belong in the trash, as well as balloons. The same goes for items with mixed materials, such as toothbrushes and disposable razors.

Be careful with black plastic containers. Many recycling programs don't accept black packaging. That's because the facilities rely on near-infrared equipment to separate plastic containers in line with their resin compositions, and these devices cannot detect black items.

Avoid problem items. Ceramics, garden hoses, Pyrex glassware, drinking glasses, plastic hangers, plastic toys, Styrofoam containers, packing peanuts, mirrors, windows, CDs, plastic handles, pens and markers, light bulbs, diapers, cigarette lighters, batteries, and toothpaste tubes should not be placed in recycling bins.

Be careful with plastic-coated paper. Check with your local recycling program to make sure that they recycle milk and food cartons, as well as juice boxes. This type of packaging tends to have low recycling rates because it is expensive to separate the paper from the plastic coating that makes it water-resistant.

Rinsing containers and removing labels is usually a good idea. Keep plastic caps on bottles and remove the lids from glass jars.

Ask your local recycling program, if you're not sure about something.

And remember:

"IF IN DOUBT, THROW IT OUT."

TerraCycle: Eliminating the Idea of Waste

When it comes to recycling, TerraCycle has done it all.

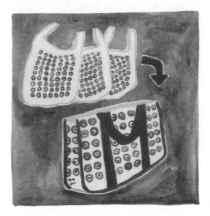

Founded by Tom Szaky and Jon Beyer in 2001, this New Jersey–based company began by turning food waste into an organic fertilizer called Worm Poop.

It later made reusable bags for Target and upcycled packaging for some of the world's best-known brands, including Oreo and Chips Ahoy, into products such as pencil cases and tote bags.

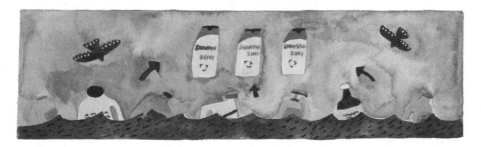

TerraCycle developed a program to turn cigarette filters into pellets that are then melted to make shipping pallets, benches, water cans, and more.

It also helped develop a shampoo bottle made of 25 percent recycled beach plastics.

TerraCycle now collects hundreds of millions of pieces of hard-to-recycle waste every year and has operations in 21 countries. It recycles latex gloves, used chewing gum, food pouches, razors, coffee pods and capsules, water filters, contact lenses, baby car seats—you name it. It even has a program to upcycle oral care products into playgrounds.

In 2019, TerraCycle launched Loop, a company that delivers products to customers in reusable containers. Once buyers use the content, Loop picks up the containers and reuses them. Loop is available in the U.K., France, and the U.S. but plans to expand to Canada, Japan, Australia, and Germany.

"The first and most important thing that citizens can do is buy less. That's way more important than recycling. Limit how much you consume. Consuming things is what creates every environmental problem in the world. [Everything] from global warming to deforestation is all linked to buying stuff."

—TerraCycle CEO Tom Szaky

Electronic Waste

The average smartphone contains metals that weigh about 3.5 ounces. That may not sound like a lot, but to source those metals, 75 pounds of rocks have to be extracted from the earth. Multiply that by the 1.4 billion new smartphones produced every year, and you get an idea of how much mining is needed to quench our thirst for new smartphones. Also, smartphones and other electronic products are typically produced in places that depend heavily on coal for energy generation, such as China, Vietnam, and Hong Kong.

Worldwide, only about 17 percent of the nearly 54 million metric tons of electronics discarded every year gets recycled. That's bad. Electronic gadgets are cool, but many contain toxic metals, such as lead, mercury, cadmium, and chromium, that can leak into groundwater and soil, poisoning the ecosystem. They also contain valuable minerals, such as aluminum, copper, lithium, and even gold. Sourcing metals from used electronics, a practice known as urban mining, has a smaller carbon footprint than extracting, processing, and transporting raw materials.

The good news is that disposing of old computers, TV sets, and smartphones in an environmentally friendly way is easy. If they are in good working condition, you can try reselling or donating them. Many large retailers also collect unwanted electronics and send them to recyclers. You can drop them at an e-waste warehouse, where technicians may try to refurbish them, extract pieces that could be used to repair other devices, or send them to recycling centers.

Of course, the best way to reduce the carbon footprint associated with electronics is to buy less and to use them until the end of their lifetimes. That's especially the case with smartphones, which can often last around five years. In the U.S. and Europe, however, people typically use their phones for a little over two years.

Things You Can Do
to reduce your bathroom's environmental footprint

Switch your toothbrush. Instead of a plastic toothbrush, go for one made with recycled plastic or bamboo.

Choose bars of soap and shampoo over liquid versions.

Don't use a disposable razor. Hundreds of millions of disposable razors every year end up in the landfill, sometimes after being used just once. Buy a reusable razor instead.

Make sure the products you buy don't contain microbeads, which are often added to facial scrubs, toothpaste, and body washes. Because these tiny pieces of polyethylene plastic are too small to be filtered by water treatment plants, they often end up in the ocean, where they are ingested by marine animals.

Look for biodegradable packaging. Several start-ups offer deodorants in biodegradable tubes, while others sell mouthwash, toothpaste tablets, and biodegradable floss in reusable containers.

Read the ingredients. Body lotions, gels, shampoos, lipstick, mascara, cleansers, and moisturizers often contain petroleum byproducts. Natural cosmetics tend to have a smaller carbon footprint because they are made with biodegradable materials.

Boycott palm oil! Palm oil is a popular ingredient in cosmetics, but its production is linked to deforestation in East Asian countries with rich biodiversity, like Indonesia and Malaysia.

Buy green cleaning products.
Choose a biodegradable bathroom cleaner instead of one made with petrochemicals. Some brands come in refillable containers—whenever you need more cleaning liquid, you can swing by one of their stores to get a refill.

Choose sunscreens wisely.
Many popular sunscreens feature chemicals such as oxybenzone and octinoxate that can damage marine life, especially corals. Mineral sunscreens containing zinc oxide or titanium dioxide are more reef-friendly.

Trees Down the Drain

The average American uses three rolls of toilet paper each week. Annually, that would cover the length of a football field 23 times.

If you buy toilet rolls made with virgin paper, there's a chance the pulp used to make them came from forests that provide habitat to wildlife while removing carbon dioxide from the atmosphere and storing it underground. Some of the largest toilet paper producers in the U.S.—including Procter & Gamble, Kimberly-Clark, and Georgia-Pacific—source paper from Canadian forests. Using these products means that when we flush toilet paper, we are literally flushing trees down the toilet.

Toilet paper made from trees has three times the climate impact of toilet paper manufactured using recycled materials.

Look for rolls made with recycled paper or alternative materials, like bamboo, that have a smaller carbon footprint. But not all bamboo rolls are the same. Choose a brand with a forest certification to ensure that farmers are not clearing forest land to grow bamboo or using unsustainable farming techniques.

And when it comes to paper towels, more often than not a reusable rag will do the work just fine.

Sara's #PlasticFreePeriod

Over the past few years, I have been thinking about the waste that builds up every month from menstrual products. When I head to the store, the choice is limited to mainly pads and tampons produced by large brands—the ones that have been accused of using chemicals that can potentially cause bacterial infections and even toxic shock syndrome, which can be fatal. I've been using these products since I was in my early teens. Recently, there's been a lot of negative media coverage about how bad regular pads and tampons are for the environment and our bodies. Women typically use thousands of these items during their lifetimes, and, once used, they end up in the landfill.

Pads and tampons have lots of plastic components. Tampon applicators and cords are typically made of plastic or synthetic materials, while tampons and pads both feature a thin layer of polyethylene and are individually wrapped in plastic. Like other single-use products, many of them end up in the ocean. Research shows that there is an average of nine plastic tampon applicators per kilometer on UK beaches.

Increasingly, my friends have been mentioning reusable options that are friendly to both the environment and women's bodies. As I've tried some reusable menstrual products, I've discovered that they help me slash the amount of waste I generate and also save me substantial amounts of cash. When I was using regular tampons and pads, I was spending around $15 a month, or $180 a year. If I menstruate for around 40 years, that's $7,200 in a lifetime! Of course, finding the right menstrual product takes some trial and error, but there are lots of choices.

MENSTRUAL CUPS. These are the best reusable option. They can be a bit messy, and placing them correctly takes a bit of practice. Menstrual cups come in different shapes and sizes, so choosing the right one for you may involve a bit of research. Some of my friends say that once you push through the initial stages of awkwardness, menstrual cups are the best thing since sliced bread!

PERIOD PANTS. These are reusable ultra-absorbent underwear. They are typically made with organic cotton and have some cool designs. All I hear is good things, except for the extra laundry. I have just ordered my first pair, and I can't wait to try them out.

REUSABLE PADS. I had the pleasure of working with a company in India called Eco Femme. They make cloth pads from cotton and donate menstrual products to women across India. They were kind enough to send me some sample products that I've loved. They are comfortable and very absorbent. Reusable pads do need to be washed, though, which can be inconvenient when traveling.

ORGANIC PADS AND TAMPONS. These are my go-to for convenience when I'm traveling. Although they are not reusable and cost more than the regular ones, at least I know that they are free of petrochemicals and will eventually biodegrade once disposed.

The Fashion Industry

If you want to reduce your carbon footprint, peek inside your closet. Chances are that it contains a fancy jacket that you never wear and a torn pair of jeans that you got ten years ago but you can't part ways with because they are just the perfect fit.

Low carbon footprint

High carbon footprint

We buy lots of clothes. Worldwide, the average person purchases approximately 25 pounds of textiles every year—the equivalent of 11 pairs of jeans and 13 T-shirts.

Fast fashion is king in the U.S. The average American buys about 83 pounds of apparel every year. Europeans buy 69 pounds, whereas Chinese citizens buy just 2.4 pounds.

THE PRODUCTION OF THOSE CLOTHES GENERATES A LOT OF CARBON DIOXIDE:

United States
3,200 pounds of carbon dioxide per person, per year

European Union
2,700 pounds

Global average
975 pounds

China
92 pounds

According to the United Nations, **the fashion industry is responsible for around 10 percent of the world's greenhouse gas emissions.** In addition, clothing manufacturers use large quantities of water and chemicals for the dyeing and finishing processes. T-shirts, socks, and shirts are typically made from cotton, a very thirsty crop that requires lots of pesticides. The polyester, nylon, and Lycra (spandex) used to make raincoats, swimwear, and leggings are derived from petrochemicals and are not biodegradable,

Fast Fashion versus Slow Fashion

THE FAST FASHION INDUSTRY

24 COLLECTIONS A YEAR

encourages users to buy several outfits every season

sells cheap clothes that don't last

pays textile workers low wages and forces them to work long hours in appalling conditions

generates waste. Every second, the equivalent of one garbage truck of textiles is landfilled or burned

SLOW FASHION CONSUMERS

choose high-quality items that last

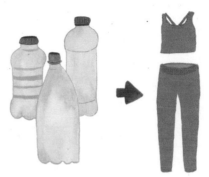

buy clothes made with organic or recycled materials

know that vintage is cool

host clothing swaps as an eco-friendly way to refresh their wardrobes

The Carbon Footprint of Your Shoes

A 2018 study found that manufacturing a single pair of shoes is linked to nearly 73 pounds of carbon dioxide emissions. Americans buy an average of seven pairs of shoes a year, which translates into approximately 500 pounds of carbon dioxide a year per person.

The main reason why shoes have a large carbon footprint is that they require a lot of manufacturing. Shoes are typically made up of dozens of parts that need to go through hundreds of manufacturing processes before they are assembled.

These processes are very energy-intensive and take place mostly in China, the world's leading footwear manufacturer. More than 90 percent of the shoes sold in the U.S. are made in China. As well as being a manufacturing powerhouse, China depends heavily on coal for energy generation.

On top of that, the sourcing of raw materials, transportation, and packaging also generate emissions.

If you want to slash the carbon footprint of your shoes, choose footwear made in places that are less dependent on coal for energy generation, like the U.S. or the E.U. You can also go for shoes with a streamlined design or those made with recycled or biodegradable materials—some brands make shoes with fennel, algae; and recycled chewing gum. Also, it's worth bearing in mind that leather shoes have a larger carbon footprint than those made with synthetic materials.

Sydney Brown

Vegan shoemaker and the founder of Sydney Brown shoes

I grew up on the outskirts of Detroit, where there were a lot of slaughterhouses. We could hear the animals screaming as we drove by, so my whole family, we all became vegetarian. Years later, after studying spirituality, I started examining leather and thinking that it was disgusting to me to be wearing animal skins. That's how I decided to stop wearing leather.

Since there were no beautiful shoes made sustainably and without leather, I decided to make my own. I took a shoemaking course and I apprenticed with an old shoemaker for about a year.

I started my company in 2011, and when we launched the first collection, we were told vegan shoes would never sell well. But people are becoming more conscious about sustainability as the climate gets worse.

Now we sell shoes all over the world, but especially in Japan. When I was twenty-five, I moved to Japan to do a master's program. Japanese spirituality influenced me very strongly. They perceive that there's a god or a spirit in all objects, inanimate objects, living objects—mountains, rocks, rivers, everything has its own spirit. Japanese design is very minimal and puts an emphasis on the materials. That's very important for me, too.

Back then most leather-less shoes were made with plastic; I didn't want to put more plastic in the world, so I started experimenting with materials. We began harvesting cork in Portugal and bonding it to cotton, and then we tried with materials like pineapple, apple, and fennel. But these materials don't bend like leather, so we had to reinvent how shoes are made. We took shoes apart, found that on average they consist of fifteen materials, and tried to produce each of them from plants. I had no idea how challenging the process would be. We could not find glues free of animal fat, so we developed our own. Now our shoes are a hundred percent vegan and made with sustainable materials.

"If we stop producing shoes today, nothing will happen. There are enough shoes out there in the world to last us probably until the end of time."

The Paper Problem

What do toilet paper, junk mail, mystery novels, and napkins have in common? They are all made out of paper. Worldwide, the paper industry produces an average of 121 pounds of paper per person every year, but that number is much higher for people living in industrialized nations, especially in North America, where per person consumption is four times higher than the global average.

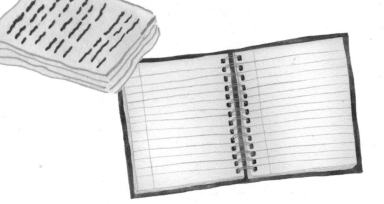

Paper use is steadily increasing, driven by the packaging and tissue industries. More demand means more production. That's bad news for the environment because paper production is energy and water intensive. And, of course, to produce paper, manufacturers have to cut down lots of trees. About a third of the global timber harvest is used to make paper.

Manufacturers in places like Indonesia, Brazil, Mozambique, and Canada often rely on pulpwood plantations that displace native forests. When native forests are cut down, the greenhouse gases stored underground are released. And pulpwood plantations don't absorb as much carbon dioxide as old-growth forests.

Trees remove CO_2 from the atmosphere and convert it into organic carbon.

Trees produce oxygen via photosynthesis and release it into the atmosphere.

Organic carbon is stored in the soil and root systems.

THE BEST WAYS TO HELP MINIMIZE THE ENVIRONMENTAL IMPACTS OF YOUR PAPER USE ARE TO REDUCE CONSUMPTION AND USE AS MUCH RECYCLED PAPER AS POSSIBLE.

Things You Can Do
to reduce your carbon footprint from paper

Buy books printed on recycled paper or Forest Stewardship Council Certified paper. Buying used books is even better. E-books are also a good option, but e-readers and tablets have myriad components and manufacturing them is energy intensive. By far the most sustainable way to read books is to borrow them from a public library.

Sign up for paperless billing. In the U.S., the average home receives nine paper bills per month, which adds up to about 13.4 billion bills a year. Choosing paperless billing for your utility bills will help you cut your greenhouse gas emissions.

Choose an electronic receipt when you shop or withdraw cash from an ATM. Paper receipts are not recyclable because they are printed on thermal paper, which contains chemicals such as bisphenol A, a hormone disruptor, that can contaminate recycled paper. Believe it or not, more than 10 million trees are downed every year to produce receipts in the U.S. alone.

Stop the stream of junk mail. More often than not, junk mail goes directly from the mailbox to the trash bin. If you live in the U.S., there are websites you can use to stop receiving junk mail, such as www.optoutprescreen.com and www.dmachoice.org. Also, adding a "No Junk Mail" sign may keep some unsolicited mail away from your mailbox.

Things You Can Do
to shop in an environmentally friendly way

Buy things that last. Consider buying things made with craftsmanship. High-quality cookware, garments, and furniture are often expensive, but they tend to have a longer lifespan. Besides, if you buy an item you really like, you're more likely to keep it longer. High-quality products can be repaired when they break, and it's easier to find buyers for them.

A steel moka pot will be your faithful companion for years on end.

Cast iron pans last a lifetime.

Sturdy dining tables are often passed down for generations.

Steel silverware is more long-lasting than the alternative.

Heavy-duty pots might be expensive, but they can last for decades.

Buy recycled products. A myriad of companies produce everyday objects made with recycled materials. The list is ever-growing, but nowadays you can easily find all these things made partially or entirely with recycled materials:

made with recycled ocean waste

made with recycled PET bottles

made with recycled fishing nets

made with recycled car tires

made with recycled milk jugs

Less Is More

Before you buy something, ask yourself, "Do I really need this? Or can I use something that I already have for the same task?" Get creative.

Use newspapers or catalogs to wrap presents.

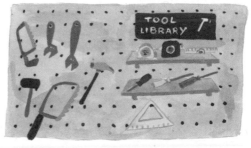

Borrow from neighbors, family, and places like tool libraries.

Make your own stuff.

If it ain't broke, **don't buy** a new one.

Refresh or upgrade old things to give them a new life.

Swap things with your friends and neighbors.

Try to fix things when they break.

The Second Life of Things

Unwanted things can have many lives.

Give them
to friends
and family.

Donate used books to bookstores.
Even better, you could set up a Little
Free Library outside your home or in
your local park.

Organize a sidewalk sale.

Leave things outside your door for others to take.

Sell them online or send a message to your social media contacts to see if someone wants them. There are a number of websites you can use to give things away, like Craigslist.

Donate them to community organizations like homeless shelters, thrift stores, and animal shelters.

Buy secondhand stuff. Help close the circle.

Things You Can Do
to bring systemic change

Fighting climate change is not only about making lifestyle changes. The fossil fuel industry is largely to blame for the climate crisis because it has deceived people by pretending that coal, oil, and natural gas do not cause global warming, even though it has known that to be the case for decades. Power companies could have switched to renewable energy long ago but instead decided to continue burning dirty fossil fuels, and carmakers could have transitioned to electric vehicles but chose to sell larger, more polluting cars in order to make more money. Politicians, meanwhile, keep issuing distant—and vague—emission-reduction targets that they rarely meet. They also have long given taxpayer money to fossil fuel companies. Lifestyle changes can help reduce emissions, but to move toward a zero-carbon future we need to hold these bigger actors accountable and force them to ditch fossil fuels. For that, we need to engage in collective efforts that have stronger ripple effects.

Join street protests.

Vote for politicians who support clean energy policies.

Call your representatives to demand climate action, and use social media to denounce polluters.

PROTECT OUR HOME

Join forces with your neighbors and work colleagues. Community will make you stronger!

DIVEST FROM FOSSIL FUELS

Divest from fossil fuels.

Donate to environmental organizations that fight for a cleaner future.

spread the word

Talk about climate solutions with family and friends.

Plant a tree.

SUPER PRACTICES

Reducing your carbon footprint is a journey as much as it is a destination, and every small step matters. But if you want to really leap forward, these are the Things You Can Do that make the biggest difference.

ENERGY

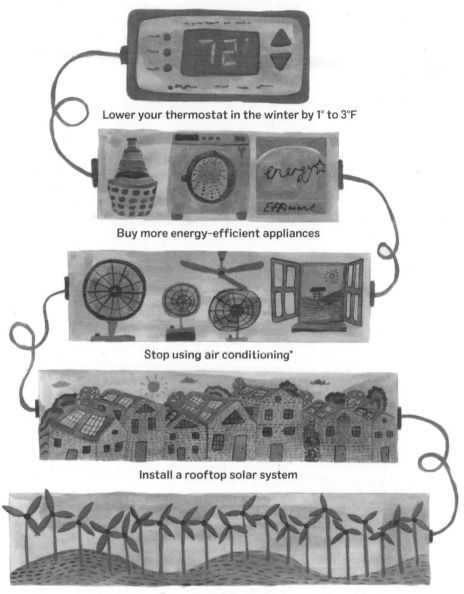

Lower your thermostat in the winter by 1° to 3°F

Buy more energy-efficient appliances

Stop using air conditioning*

Install a rooftop solar system

Buy renewable energy

*Refurbishing your home to make it energy-efficient or switching from oil or gas heating to electric heating leads to similar carbon reductions.

FOOD

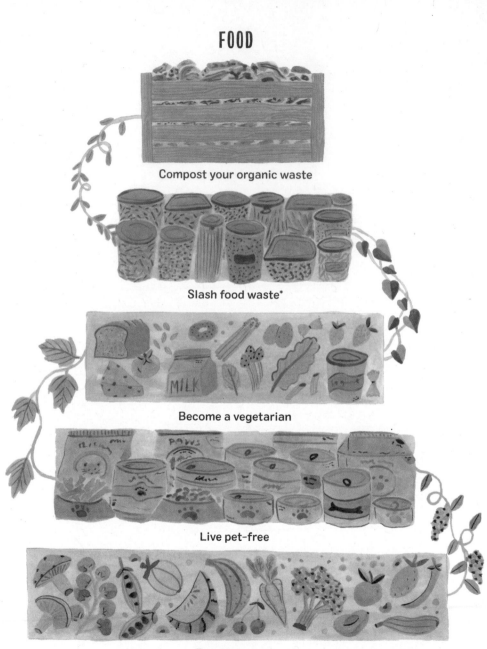

Compost your organic waste

Slash food waste*

Become a vegetarian

Live pet-free

Become vegan

*Buying organic fruits and vegetables from local farmers instead of from supermarkets will have a similar effect.

TRANSPORTATION

Practice eco-driving

Avoid trips by car under three miles

Avoid flying

Drive a budget electric vehicle

Live car-free

WASTE

Shop less, reuse, refurbish, donate, and buy more durable things

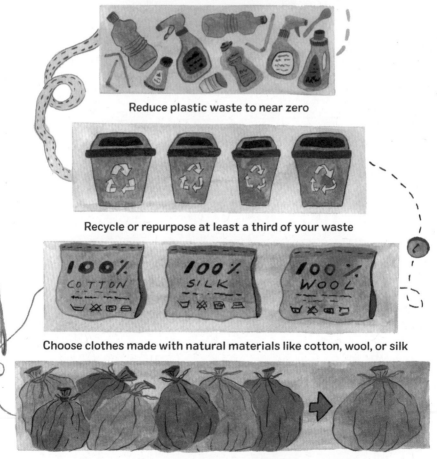

Reduce plastic waste to near zero

Recycle or repurpose at least a third of your waste

Choose clothes made with natural materials like cotton, wool, or silk

Slash the amount of waste you create by at least 75%

RESOURCES

If you want to dig deeper, these are some websites where you can find data and reports to learn about key topics, as well as additional tips to help you slash your carbon footprint.

CLIMATE CHANGE

Copernicus Climate Change Service: *The European Union's climate website.* climate.copernicus.eu

Global Carbon Project: *Up-to-date climate data and analysis.* www.globalcarbonproject.org

NASA Global Climate Change: *NASA's climate portal.* climate.nasa.gov

National Oceanic and Atmospheric Administration (NOAA): *Scientific data and reports about the Earth's atmosphere and oceans.* www.noaa.gov

Project Drawdown: *Your go-to source for information on climate solutions.* https://drawdown.org/

Union of Concerned Scientists: *Nonprofit science advocacy organization that supports renewable energy and clean transport.* www.ucsusa.org

United Nations Environment Programme: *The UN office for environmental issues.* www.unep.org

US Environmental Protection Agency: *Information on US greenhouse gas emissions and pollution.* www.epa.gov

ELECTRICITY

Energy Star: *How to save energy at home.* www.energystar.gov/products/energy_star_home_tips

International Energy Agency: *Up-to-date statistics from the IEA, the global authority on energy.* www.iea.org

International Renewable Energy Agency: *Reports and data from IRENA, an organization that promotes sustainable energy.* www.irena.org

Natural Resources Defense Council: *Advice on how to live sustainably from NRDC, a nonprofit fighting to preserve nature.* www.nrdc.org/story/personal-action

US Department of Energy: *Tips on how to improve your home's energy efficiency.* www.energy.gov/eere/energy-efficiency

US Environmental Protection Agency: *A database of rebates to help US homeowners upgrade their homes.* lookforwatersense.epa.gov/rebates

US Environmental Protection Agency: *A guide to purchasing green power.* www.epa.gov/greenpower/guide-purchasing-green-power

FOOD

Animal Welfare Institute: *Nonprofit fighting for animal rights.* awionline.org

Cummings School of Veterinary Medicine at Tufts University: *Information about the carbon footprint of pet food and tips on how to feed your pet a sustainable diet.* vetnutrition.tufts.edu/2018/02/petfood_sustainability

EAT-Lancet Commission on Food, Planet, Health: *A one-stop source for information on sustainable diets.* eatforum.org/eat-lancet-commission

Environmental Working Group: *Nonprofit specializing in agriculture, pollution, and corporate accountability that publishes The Dirty Dozen, a shopper's guide to pesticides in produce.* www.ewg.org

Food and Agriculture Organization: *The global authority on food and agriculture has up-to-date data and in-depth reports.* www.fao.org /about/en

Humane Society: *Nonprofit advocating for animal rights.* www.humanesociety.org

Institute for Local Self-Reliance: *This sustainability nonprofit has plenty of information on composting.* ilsr.org

Local Harvest: *A website to help you find farmers markets nearby.* www.localharvest.org

Nature Conservancy: *This global environmental organization frequently publishes reports about agricultural production, biodiversity, and clean energy.* www.nature.org/en-us

NOAA Fisheries: *Promotes sustainable fisheries and protects the United States' ocean resources.* www.fisheries.noaa.gov

Regenerative Organic Alliance: *Promotes regenerative agriculture.* regenorganic.org

Rob Greenfield: *Videos, posts, and tips from a green-living expert.* www.robgreenfield.org

Rodale Institute: *A nonprofit dedicated to growing the organic movement.* rodaleinstitute.org

Seafood Watch: *A global leader in the sustainable seafood movement that publishes a guide to help consumers buy sustainable seafood.* www.seafoodwatch.org

Seasonal Food Guide: *Find what is in season near you.* www.seasonalfoodguide.org

Zero Footprint: *A nonprofit organization mobilizing the food world around agricultural climate solutions.* www.zerofoodprint.org

TRANSPORTATION

Flight Free World: *To find out more about the Flight Free campaign.* flightfree.world

Frontier Group: *Nonprofit promoting clean energy and green forms of transportation.* frontiergroup.org

Institute for Transportation and Development Policy: *Nonprofit that promotes public transportation, biking, and walking.* www.itdp.org

International Civil Aviation Organization: *This UN office has up-to-date data and reports about air transportation.* icao.int

International Council on Clean Transportation: *Promotes low-carbon forms of transportation.* theicct.org

Shared-Use Mobility Center: *Nonprofit that promotes shared forms of transportation.* sharedusemobilitycenter.org

The Transport Politic: *A website about urban transportation.* www.thetransportpolitic.com

Transport and the Environment: *Works to expose the impact of transport on our climate, environment, and health.* www.transportenvironment.org

US Department of Energy Fuel Economy: *For information on how to increase your car's mileage.* www.fueleconomy.gov

WASTE

Ellen MacArthur Foundation: *News and reports about the circular economy.* www.ellenmacarthurfoundation.org

Environmental Paper Network: *Organization that promotes sustainable paper production.* environmentalpaper.org

Food Packaging Forum: *A one-stop website for information on food packaging and its impact on human health and the environment.* www.foodpackagingforum.org

Going Zero Waste: *Tips on how to reduce waste from zero-waste personality Kathryn Kellogg.* www.goingzerowaste.com

Green America: *Nonprofit promoting environmental awareness.* www.greenamerica.org

Litterless: *A zero-waste grocery guide for people living in the U.S.* www.litterless.com/wheretoshop

Sustainable Jungle: *News and tips about sustainable living.* www.sustainablejungle.com

Trash Is for Tossers: *An editorial platform by blogger and entrepreneur Lauren Singer to help you move toward a low- or zero-waste lifestyle.* trashisfortossers.com

Waste Management: *This leading waste management company has a checklist to help you recycle effectively.* www.wm.com/us/en/recycle-right/recycling-101

Zero-Waste Chef: *A website dedicated to zero-waste cooking and plant-forward recipes to help you reduce your kitchen's carbon footprint.* zerowastechef.com

SOURCES

INTRODUCTION ·

Inspired by "the hummingbird tale," as told by the late Kenyan environmental activist and Nobel Laureate, Wangari Maathai.

CHAPTER ONE ·

Arizona State University. *World Highest Temperature.* World Meteorological Organization's World Weather and Climate Extremes Archive. wmo.asu.edu /content/world-highest-temperature

Arizona State University. *World Lowest Temperature.* World Meteorological Organization's World Weather and Climate Extremes Archive. wmo.asu.edu /content/world-lowest-temperature

Cambridge University. 2020. *Jane Goodall: Finding Our Way to a Better Future.* youtu.be/ZIzRWqORVIU

Carrington, D. 2020. Christiana Figueres on the climate emergency: 'This is the decade and we are the generation.' *The Guardian.* bit.ly/3cZxwDu

Copernicus. 2021. *2020 Warmest Year on Record for Europe; Globally, 2020 Ties with 2016 for Warmest Year Recorded.* climate.copernicus.eu/copernicus-2020 -warmest-year-record-europe-globally-2020-ties-2016-warmest-year-recorded

Denchak, M. 2019. *Greenhouse Effect 101.* Natural Resources Research Council. www.nrdc.org/stories/greenhouse-effect-101

Florida Center for Environmental Studies. n.d. *Energy: The Driver of Climate.* Climate Science Investigations (CSI). www.ces.fau.edu/nasa/images/Energy /EnergyTheDriverOfClimate.pdf

Friedlingstein, P., et al. 2020. Global carbon budget 2020. *Earth Systems Science Data* 12, 3269–3340. doi: 10.5194/essd-12-3269-2020

Global Carbon Project. n.d. *The Global Carbon Atlas.* www.globalcarbonatlas .org/en/CO2-emissions

Global Carbon Project. n.d. *Global Carbon Budget 2020*. www.globalcarbon project.org/carbonbudget/20/files/GCP_CarbonBudget_2020.pdf

International Union for Conservation of Nature. n.d. *Coral Reefs and Climate Change*. www.iucn.org/resources/issues-briefs/coral-reefs-and-climate-change

IPCC. 2018. *Summary for Policymakers of IPCC Special Report on Global Warming of 1.5°C Approved by Governments*. www.ipcc.ch/2018/10/08 /summary-for-policymakers-of-ipcc-special-report-on-global-warming-of -1-5c-approved-by-governments

Ivanova, D., et al. 2020. Quantifying the potential for climate change mitigation of consumption options. *Environmental Research Letters* 15(9):093001. doi: 10.1088/1748-9326/ab8589

James, H. 1988. *Congressional Testimony of Dr. James Hansen*. Sealevl.info. www.sealevel.info/1988_Hansen_Senate_Testimony.html

NASA. n.d. *Global Climate Change*. climate.nasa.gov

NASA. 2021. *2020 Tied for Warmest Year on Record, NASA Analysis Shows*. www.nasa.gov/press-release/2020-tied-for-warmest-year-on-record-nasa -analysis-shows

NASA Earth Observatory. earthobservatory.nasa.gov/world-of-change /decadaltemp.php

NASA Earth Observatory. *Land Surface Temperature*. earthobservatory.nasa .gov/global-maps/MOD_LSTD_M

NASA Science. *Solar System Exploration*. solarsystem.nasa.gov/solar-system /our-solar-system/overview

National Oceanic and Atmospheric Administration. *Monthly Average Mauna Loa CO_2*. www.esrl.noaa.gov/gmd/ccgg/trends/mlo.html#mlo

National Oceanic and Atmospheric Administration, Lindsey, R. 2020. *Climate Change: Atmospheric Carbon Dioxide*. www.climate.gov/news-features /understanding-climate/climate-change-atmospheric-carbon-dioxide

Natural Resources Research Council, Denchak, M. 2019. *Greenhouse Effect 101*. www.nrdc.org/stories/greenhouse-effect-101

North Carolina Climate Office. *Climate Education Modules*. climate.ncsu.edu /edu/home

Public Broadcasting Service. 2020. *David Attenborough on How Our Changing Climate Affects Wildlife.* www.pbs.org/wnet/nature/blog/david-attenborough -on-how-our-changing-climate-affects-wildlife

Ritchie, H. n.d. *Who Has Contributed Most to Global CO_2 Emissions? Our World in Data.* ourworldindata.org/contributed-most-global-co2

Román-Palacios, C., Wiens, J. J. 2020. Recent responses to climate change reveal the drivers of species extinction and survival. *PNAS* 117(8): 4211–4217. doi:10.1073/pnas.1913007117

Sabine, C., et al. 2014. Ask the Experts: The IPCC Fifth Assessment Report. *Carbon Management* 5(1), 17–25. doi: 10.4155/cmt.13.80

Space.com. n.d. *Gas Giants: Facts About the Outer Planets.* www.space.com /30372-gas-giants.html

Space.com. n.d. *Terrestrial Planets: Definition & Facts About the Inner Planets.* www.space.com/17028-terrestrial-planets.html

Stevens, A. N. P. 2010. *The Nature Education Knowledge Project: Introduction to the Basic Drivers of Climate.* www.nature.com/scitable/knowledge/library /introduction-to-the-basic-drivers-of-climate-13368032

Thunberg, G. 2019. 'Our house is on fire': Greta Thunberg, 16, urges leaders to act on climate. *The Guardian.* www.theguardian.com/environment/2019/jan/25 /our-house-is-on-fire-greta-thunberg16-urges-leaders-to-act-on-climate

Union of Concerned Scientists. n.d. *Climate Impacts.* www.ucsusa.org/climate /impacts

US Environmental Protection Agency. *Carbon Footprint Calculator.* www3.epa .gov/carbon-footprint-calculator

US Environmental Protection Agency. *Overview of Greenhouse Gases.* Greenhouse Gas (GHG) Emissions. www.epa.gov/ghgemissions

US Global Change Research Program. *2014 National Climate Assessment.* nca2014.globalchange.gov/report

Vidal, J. 2009. 'We know what to do: Why don't we do it?' *The Guardian.* www.theguardian.com/environment/2009/may/30/africa-women-climate -change-wangari-maathai

World Meteorological Organization. 2020. *Carbon Dioxide Levels Continue at Record Levels, Despite COVID-19 Lockdown.* public.wmo.int/en/media/press-release/carbon-dioxide-levels-continue-record-levels-despite-covid-19-lockdown

CHAPTER TWO 💡 ·

Carbon Brief. n.d. *Mapped: The World's Coal Power Plants.* www.carbonbrief.org/mapped-worlds-coal-power-plants

Carbon Brief. 2020. *Analysis: Will China Build Hundreds of New Coal Plants in the 2020s?* www.carbonbrief.org/analysis-will-china-build-hundreds-of-new-coal-plants-in-the-2020s

Carrington, D. 2019. Only a third of world's great rivers remain free flowing, analysis finds. *The Guardian.* www.theguardian.com/environment/2019/may/08/only-a-third-of-worlds-great-rivers-remain-free-flowing-analysis-finds

Congressional Research Service, Copeland, C. 2017. *Energy-Water Nexus: The Water Sector's Energy Use.* fas.org/sgp/crs/misc/R43200.pdf

De Cian, E., et al. 2019. Households' adaptation in a warming climate: air conditioning and thermal insulation choices. *Environmental Science and Policy* 100, 133–157. doi: 10.1016/j.envsci.2019.06.015

Girod, B., et al. 2014. Climate policy through changing consumption choices: options and obstacles for reducing greenhouse gas emissions. *Global Environmental Change* 25, 5–15. doi: 10.1016/j.gloenvcha.2014.01.004

Griffiths-Sattenspiel, B., Wilson, W. 2019. The Carbon Footprint of Water. *River Network Report.* www.csu.edu/cerc/researchreports/documents/CarbonFootprintofWater-RiverNetwork-2009.pdf

IEA Clean Coal Centre. 2019. *Top Coal-Fired Power Generating Countries.* www.iea-coal.org/top-coal-fired-power-generating-countries

International Energy Agency. n.d. *Electricity Information: Overview.* www.iea.org/reports/electricity-information-overview

International Energy Agency. 2018. *Air Conditioning Use Emerges as One of the Key Drivers of Global Electricity-Demand Growth.* www.iea.org/news/air-conditioning-use-emerges-as-one-of-the-key-drivers-of-global-electricity-demand-growth

International Energy Agency. 2018. *The Future of Cooling*. www.iea.org/reports /the-future-of-cooling

International Energy Agency. 2019. *World Gross Electricity Production, by Source, 2018*. www.iea.org/data-and-statistics/charts/world-gross-electricity -production-by-source-2018

International Energy Agency. 2020. *IEA Energy Atlas*. energyatlas.iea.org/#! /tellmap/1378539487

International Renewable Energy Agency. 2021. *Renewable Energy Highlights*. www.irena.org/-/media/Files/IRENA/Agency/Publication/2020/Jul /Renewable_energy_highlights_July_2020.pdf

National Electric Power Regulatory Authority. 2021. *State of Industry Report 2020*. bit.ly/3fRUzle

Natural Resources Defense Council, Evans, L. 2019. *How to Shop for Energy-Efficient Light Bulbs*. www.nrdc.org/stories/how-shop-energy-efficient -light-bulbs

Natural Resources Research Council. 2015. Home Idle Load: Devices Wasting Huge Amounts of Electricity When Not in Active Use. *NRDC Issue Paper*. www.nrdc.org/sites/default/files/home-idle-load-IP.pdf

Reuters. 2020. *India's Annual Coal Power Output Falls for First Time in a Decade*. uk.reuters.com/article/uk-india-coal-electricity/indias-annual-coal -power-output-falls-for-first-time-in-a-decade-idUKKBN20B1I2

Reuters. 2020. *Indonesia Plans to Replace Old Coal Power Plants with Renewable Plants: Minister*. www.reuters.com/article/us-indonesia-power-coal /indonesia-plans-to-replace-old-coal-power-plants-with-renewable-plants -minister-idUSKBN1ZT17N

Union of Concerned Scientists. n.d. *Benefits of Renewable Energy Use*. www.ucsusa.org/resources/benefits-renewable-energy-use

Union of Concerned Scientists. n.d. *Environmental Impacts of Natural Gas*. ucsusa.org/resources/environmental-impacts-natural-gas

US Department of Energy. *Lighting Choices to Save You Money*. www.energy .gov/energysaver/save-electricity-and-fuel/lighting-choices-save-you-money

US Energy Information Administration. n.d. Electricity Explained: *How Electricity Is Generated.* www.eia.gov/energyexplained/electricity/how-electricity-is-generated.php

US Energy Information Administration. n.d. *Electricity Explained: Use of Electricity.* www.eia.gov/energyexplained/electricity/use-of-electricity.php

US Energy Information Administration. n.d. *What Is U.S. Electricity Generation by Energy Source?* www.eia.gov/tools/faqs/faq.php?id=427&t=3

US Energy Information Administration. 2018. *Air Conditioning Accounts for About 12% of U.S. Home Energy Expenditures.* www.eia.gov/todayinenergy/detail.php?id=36692#

US Energy Information Administration. 2021. *How Is Electricity Used in U.S. Homes?* www.eia.gov/tools/faqs/faq.php?id=96&t=3

US Environmental Protection Agency. n.d. *James H. Miller Jr.: 2018.* ghgdata.epa.gov/ghgp/service/facilityDetail/2018?id=1007227&ds=E&et=&popup=true

US Environmental Protection Agency. 2020. *Greenhouse Gas Equivalencies Calculator.* www.epa.gov/energy/greenhouse-gas-equivalencies-calculator

The World Bank. n.d. *Electric Power Consumption (kWh per capita).* data.worldbank.org/indicator/EG.USE.ELEC.KH.PC?most_recent_value_desc=true

The World Bank. n.d. *Electric Power Consumption (kWh per capita).* data.worldbank.org/indicator/EG.USE.ELEC.KH.PC?view=chart

CHAPTER THREE

Animal Welfare Institute. n.d. *Farm Animals.* awionline.org/content/farm-animals

Carbon Brief, Dunne, D. 2020. *Nitrogen Fertiliser Use Could 'Threaten Global Climate Goals'.* www.carbonbrief.org/nitrogen-fertiliser-use-could-threaten-global-climate-goals

Carrington, D., Carrington, D. 2018. Humans just 0.01% of all life but have destroyed 83% of wild mammals: study. *The Guardian.* www.theguardian.com/environment/2018/may/21/human-race-just-001-of-all-life-but-has-destroyed-over-80-of-wild-mammals-study

Cohen, P. 2020. Roundup maker to pay $10 billion to settle cancer suits. *New York Times.* www.nytimes.com/2020/06/24/business/roundup-settlement-lawsuits.html

Drawdown. n.d. *Regenerative Annual Cropping.* www.drawdown.org/solutions/regenerative-annual-cropping

The EAT-Lancet Commission. 2019. *Healthy Diets from Sustainable Food Systems: Food Planet Health.* eatforum.org/content/uploads/2019/07/EAT-Lancet_Commission_Summary_Report.pdf

Ellen MacArthur Foundation. 2019. *Cities and Circular Economy for Food.* www.ellenmacarthurfoundation.org/assets/downloads/Cities-and-Circular-Economy-for-Food_280119.pdf

Environmental Defense Fund. n.d. *Consumer Food Waste: Solutions.* supplychain.edf.org/resources/consumer-food-waste-solutions

FAO. n.d. *Gateway to Poultry Production and Products: Chicken.* www.fao.org/poultry-production-products/production/poultry-species/chickens/en

FAO. n.d. *GLEAM 2.0: Assessment of Greenhouse Gas Emissions and Mitigation Potential.* Global Livestock Environmental Assessment Model (GLEAM). www.fao.org/gleam/results/en

FAO. 2018. *Beauty (and Taste!) Are on the Inside.* www.fao.org/fao-stories/article/en/c/1100391

FAO. 2020. *The State of World Fisheries and Aquaculture: World Review.* www.fao.org/3/ca9229en/online/ca9229en.html#chapter-1_1

Graham, J. n.d. *Tillage Destroys Soil's Physical Properties.* www.nrcs.usda.gov/wps/portal/nrcs/detail/ky/soils/?cid=stelprdb1096792

Gustin, G. 2019. *As Beef Comes Under Fire for Climate Impacts, the Industry Fights Back.* insideclimatenews.org/news/21102019/climate-change-meat-beef-dairy-methane-emissions-california

Harvard T.H. Chan School of Public Health. n.d. *The Nutrition Source: Legumes and Pulses.* www.hsph.harvard.edu/nutritionsource/legumes-pulses

Humane Society, Smith, E. 2019. *Do You Really Know How Most Farm Animals Live?* www.humanesociety.org/news/do-you-really-know-how-most-farm-animals-live

Institute for Local Self-Reliance. n.d. *Home Composting Basics*. ilsr.org/home
-composting-basics

International Center for Research on Cancer. 2015. *IARC Monograph on
Glyphosate*. www.iarc.who.int/featured-news/media-centre-iarc-news
-glyphosate

Johnson, E. 2009. Charcoal versus LPG grilling: a carbon-footprint comparison.
Environmental Impact Assessment Review 29(6), 370–378. doi: 10.1016/j
.eiar.2009.02.004

Martens, P., et al. 2019. The ecological paw print of companion dogs and cats.
BioScience 69(6), 467–474. doi: 10.1093/biosci/biz044

McGivney, A. 2020. Almonds are out. dairy is a disaster. so what milk should
we drink? *The Guardian*. www.theguardian.com/environment/2020/jan/28
/what-plant-milk-should-i-drink-almond-killing-bees-aoe

Monterrey Bay Aquarium. n.d. *Seafood Watch*. www.seafoodwatch.org

NASA. n.d. *Which Is a Bigger Methane Source: Cow Belching or Cow Flatulence?*
climate.nasa.gov/faq/33/which-is-a-bigger-methane-source-cow-belching-or
-cow-flatulence

Native Seeds/SEARCH, Kruse-Peeples, M. How to Grow a Three Sisters Garden,
Education Coordinator. www.nativeseeds.org/blogs/blog-news/how-to-grow-
a-three-sisters-garden

Nature Conservancy. 2020. *The Global Food System Is Ripe for Change*.
www.nature.org/en-us/what-we-do/our-insights/perspectives/grow-positive-
regenerative-global-food-system

NOAA Fisheries. n.d. *Species Directory*. www.fisheries.noaa.gov/species-directory

OECD and FAO. 2020. *OECD-FAO Agricultural Outlook 2020–2029*. doi:
10.1787/1112c23b-en

Okin, G. 2017. Environmental Impacts of Food Consumption by Dogs and Cats.
Plos One 12(8): e0181301. doi: 10.1371/journal.pone.0181301

Peter, A., et al. 2016. Human Appropriation of Land for Food: The Role of Diet.
Global Environmental Change 41, 88–98. doi: 10.1016/j.gloenvcha.2016.09.005

Poore, J., Nemecek, T. 2018. Reducing Food's Environmental Impacts through Producers and Consumers. *Science* 360(6392), 987–992. doi: 10.1126/science.aaq0216

Regenerative Organic Alliance. 2021. *Framework for Regenerative Organic Certified.* regenorganic.org/wp-content/uploads/2021/02/ROC_ROC_STD_FR_v5.pdf

Ritchie, H., Max, R. 2020. *Environmental Impacts of Food Production.* ourworldindata.org/environmental-impacts-of-food

Sulaeman, D., Westhoff, T. 2020. *The Causes and Effects of Soil Erosion, and How to Prevent It.* www.wri.org/blog/2020/01/causes-effects-how-to-prevent-soil-erosion

WWF. 2016. *What's the Environmental Impact of Pet Food?* www.worldwildlife.org/magazine/issues/spring-2016/articles/what-s-the-environmental-impact-of-pet-food

CHAPTER FOUR

American Oil and Gas Historical Society. n.d. *First Car, First Road Trip.* www.aoghs.org/transportation/benz-patents-first-car

American Public Transport Association. n.d. *Public Transportation Facts.* www.apta.com/news-publications/public-transportation-facts

American School Bus Council. n.d. *School Bus Facts: The Benefits of School Bus Ridership.* schoolbusfacts.com/resources

Bureau of Transport Statistics. n.d. *Number of U.S. Aircraft, Vehicles, Vessels, and Other Conveyances.* www.bts.gov/content/number-us-aircraft-vehicles-vessels-and-other-conveyances

Carbon Brief, Lee, D., Forster, P. n.d. *Calculating the True Climate Impact of Aviation Emissions.* www.carbonbrief.org/guest-post-calculating-the-true-climate-impact-of-aviation-emissions

European Commission. n.d. *How Many People Can You Reach by Public Transport, Bicycle or on Foot in European Cities?* Measuring *Urban Accessibility for Low-Carbon Modes.* ec.europa.eu/regional_policy/en/information/maps/low-carbon-urban-accessibility

Ford. n.d. *The Model T.* corporate.ford.com/articles/history/the-model-t.html

Frontier Group. 2020. *Destination: Zero Carbon.* frontiergroup.org/sites/default /files/reports/AME%20Zero%20Carbon%20Report%20Jan20-web.pdf

Frontier Group. 2021. *Transform Transportation.* frontiergroup.org/reports/fg /transform-transportation

International Civil Aviation Organization. n.d. *The World of Air Transport in 2019.* www.icao.int/annual-report-2019/Pages/the-world-of-air-transport-in-2019.aspx

International Council on Clean Transportation. n.d. *CO2 Emissions from Commercial Aviation, 2018.* theicct.org/publications/co2-emissions-commercial -aviation-2018

International Council on Clean Transportation, Rutherford, D. 2019. *Need to Fly? Fly Like a NERD!* theicct.org/blog/staff/fly-like-a-nerd-20191028

International Energy Agency. n.d. *World Energy Outlook 2019.* www.iea.org /reports/world-energy-outlook-2019

International Energy Agency. 2019. *Growing Preference for SUVs Challenges Emissions Reductions in Passenger Car Market.* www.iea.org/commentaries /growing-preference-for-suvs-challenges-emissions-reductions-in-passenger -car-market

National Association of City Transportation Officials. n.d. *Shared Micromobility in the U.S.: 2019.* nacto.org/shared-micromobility-2019

Our World in Data, Ritchie, H. 2020. Sector by sector: where do global greenhouse gas emissions come from? ourworldindata.org/ghg-emissions- by-sector

Project Drawdown. n.d. *Electric Bicycles.* www.drawdown.org/solutions/electric -bicycles

Tabuchi, H. 2019. 'Worse than anyone expected': air travel emissions vastly outpace predictions. *New York Times.* www.nytimes.com/2019/09/19/climate /air-travel-emissions.html

Transport and Environment. 2020. *Does an Electric Vehicle Emit Less Than a Petrol or Diesel?* www.transportenvironment.org/news/does-electric-vehicle -emit-less-petrol-or-diesel

The Transport Politic, Freemark, Y. 2020. *Too Little, Too Late? A Decade of Transit Investment in the U.S.* www.thetransportpolitic.com/2020/01/07/too-little-too-late-a-decade-of-transit-investment-in-the-u-s

Union of Concerned Scientists. n.d. *Ride-Hailing Is a Problem for the Climate. Here's Why.* www.ucsusa.org/resources/ride-hailing-problem-climate

US Department of Energy. n.d. *Idling Reduction for Personal Vehicles.* afdc.energy.gov/files/u/publication/idling_personal_vehicles.pdf

US Department of Energy. n.d. *Where the Energy Goes: Electric Cars.* www.fueleconomy.gov/feg/atv-ev.shtml

US Department of Energy. n.d. *Where the Energy Goes: Gasoline Vehicles.* www.fueleconomy.gov/feg/atv.shtml

Voelk, T. 2020. Rise of S.U.V.s: leaving cars in their dust, with no signs of slowing. *New York Times.* www.nytimes.com/2020/05/21/business/suv-sales-best-sellers.html

World Economic Forum. 2020. *The Future of the Last-Mile Ecosystem.* www3.weforum.org/docs/WEF_Future_of_the_last_mile_ecosystem.pdf

World Health Organization. 2018. *Ambient (Outdoor) Air Pollution.* www.who.int/news-room/fact-sheets/detail/ambient-(outdoor)-air-quality-and-health

Yglesias, M. 2019. Air pollution is much more harmful than you know. *Vox.* www.vox.com/future-perfect/2019/12/11/20996968/air-pollution-cognitive-impact

CHAPTER FIVE

American Chemistry Council. 2021. *Shale Gas Is Driving New Chemical Industry Investment in the U.S.* www.americanchemistry.com/Shale_Gas_Fact_Sheet.aspx

Carbon Brief, Hausfather, Z. 2018. *Analysis: Why the IPCC 1.5C Report Expanded the Carbon Budget.* www.carbonbrief.org/analysis-why-the-ipcc-1-5c-report-expanded-the-carbon-budget

Center for International Environmental Law. 2017. *Fueling Plastics: How Fracked Gas, Cheap Oil, and Unburnable Coal Are Driving the Plastics.* www.ciel.org/wp-content/uploads/2017/09/Fueling-Plastics-How-Fracked-Gas-Cheap-Oil-and-Unburnable-Coal-are-Driving-the-Plastics-Boom.pdf

Center for International Environmental Law, Hamilton, L. A., Feit, S., et al. 2019. *Plastic and Climate: The Hidden Costs of a Plastic Planet.* www.ciel.org/wp-content/uploads/2019/05/Plastic-and-Climate-FINAL-2019.pdf

Cheah, L., et al. 2013. Manufacturing-focused emissions reductions in footwear production. *Journal of Cleaner Production.* 44,18–29. doi: org/10.1016/j.jclepro.2012.11.037

Consumer Reports. 2016. *Toilet Paper Buying Guide.* www.consumerreports.org/cro/toilet-paper/buying-guide/index.htm

Cox, K. D., et al. 2019. Human consumption of microplastics. *Environmental Science and Technology* 53(12), 7068–7074. doi: 10.1021/acs.est.9b01517

Diaz, J. 2019. Dead whale, 220 pounds of debris inside, is a 'grim reminder' of ocean trash. *New York Times.* www.nytimes.com/2019/12/02/world/europe/harris-beached-whale.html

Environmental Paper Network. *The State of the Global Paper Industry, 2018.* environmentalpaper.org/wp-content/uploads/2018/04/StateOfTheGlobalPaperIndustry2018_FullReport-Final-1.pdf

European Container Glass Federation. 2020. *Latest Glass Packaging Recycling Rate Steady at 76%.* feve.org/about-glass/statistics

Eurostat. 2021. *Municipal Waste Statistics.* ec.europa.eu/eurostat/statistics-explained/index.php/Municipal_waste_statistics#Municipal_waste_treatment

Food Packaging Forum. 2021. *Recycling of Aluminum Cans in EU Reaches 76%.* www.foodpackagingforum.org/news/recycling-of-aluminum-cans-in-eu-reaches-76

Geyer, R., et al. 2017. Production, use, and fate of all plastics ever made. *Science Advances* 3(7), e1700782. doi: 10.1126/sciadv.1700782

Green America. 2018. *Skip the Slip, Environmental Costs and Human Health Risks of Paper Receipts with Proposed Solutions.* www.greenamerica.org/sites/default/files/2018-08/Skip percent20the percent20Slip percent20Report percent20- percent20Green percent20America.pdf

Greenpeace. 2017. *Guide to Greener Electronics 2017.* Greenpeace Reports. www.greenpeace.org/usa/reports/greener-electronics-2017

Lavers, J. L., et al. 2019. Significant plastic accumulation on the Cocos (Keeling) Islands, Australia. *Scientific Reports* 9, 7102. doi: 10.1038/s41598-019-43375-4

Martinko, K. 2021. *The Right Way to Dispose of Paper Receipts.* Treehugger. www.treehugger.com/can-receipts-be-recycled-5072255

Metal Packaging Europe. n.d. *Aluminium Beverage Can Recycling in Europe Hits Record 76.1% in 2018.* www.metalpackagingeurope.org/article/aluminium -beverage-can-recycling-europe-hits-record-761-2018

Peixoto, D. 2019. Microplastic pollution in commercial salt for human consumption: a review. *Estuarine, Coastal and Shelf Science* 219(5), 161–168. doi: 10.1016/j.ecss.2019.02.018

Perkins, T. 2021. Toxic 'forever chemicals' are contaminating plastic food containers. *The Guardian.* www.theguardian.com/environment/2021/jul/09 /toxic-forever-chemicals-plastic-food-containers

PEW Charitable Trusts, Systemiq. 2020. *Breaking the Plastic Wave.* www.pewtrusts .org/-/media/assets/2020/10/breakingtheplasticwave_mainreport.pdf

Plastics Make It Possible. 2018. *Types of Plastic: How Many Kinds of Plastics Are There?* www.plasticsmakeitpossible.com/about-plastics/types-of-plastics /professor-plastics-how-many-types-of-plastics-are-there

Quantis. 2018. *Measuring Fashion: Environmental Impact of the Global Apparel and Footwear Industries Study.* quantis-intl.com/wp-content/uploads/2018/03 /measuringfashion_globalimpactstudy_full-report_quantis_cwf_2018a.pdf

Schuyler, Q. A., et al. 2016. Risk analysis reveals global hotspots for marine debris ingestion by sea turtles. *Global Change Biology* 22(2), 567–576. doi: 10.1111 /gcb.13078

Science History. n.d. *Science of Plastics.* www.sciencehistory.org/sites/default /files/science-of-plastics-2.pdf

Science History Institute. n.d. *History and Future of Plastics.* www.sciencehistory .org/the-history-and-future-of-plastics

Scottish Government. 2019. *Mapping Economic, Behavioural and Social Factors within the Plastic Value Chain that Lead to Marine Litter in Scotland.* bit.ly/3cX86WJ

SCS Global Services, Schultz, T., Suresh, A. 2018. *Life Cycle Impact Assessment Methodology for Environmental Paper Network Paper Calculator v4.0.* c.environmentalpaper.org/pdf/SCS-EPN-PC-Methods.pdf

Skene, J. and Vinyard S. NRDC. 2020. The Issue with Tissue 2.0. www.nrdc.org/sites/default/files/issue-with-tissue-2-report.pdf

Tearfund, Mari, W. 2019. *No Time to Waste: Tackling the Plastic Pollution Crisis Before It's Too Late.* www.tearfund.org/-/media/learn/resources/reports/2019-tearfund-consortium-no-time-to-waste-en.pdf

Today. 2020. Here's how much toilet paper a family of 4 needs for 2 weeks. *MSNBC/TODAY.* www.today.com/health/here-s-how-much-toilet-paper-family-4-needs-2-t176154

United Nations Environment Programme. 2019. *Is Your Phone Really Smart?* www.unep.org/news-and-stories/story/your-phone-really-smart

US Energy Information Administration. 2021. *Natural Gas Explained.* www.eia.gov/energyexplained/natural-gas/where-our-natural-gas-comes-from.php

US Environmental Protection Agency. 2020. *Advancing Sustainable Materials Management: 2018 Fact Sheet.* www.epa.gov/sites/production/files/2021-01/documents/2018_ff_fact_sheet_dec_2020_fnl_508.pdf

US Environmental Protection Agency. 2020. *Aluminum: Material-Specific Data.* www.epa.gov/facts-and-figures-about-materials-waste-and-recycling/aluminum-material-specific-data

US Environmental Protection Agency. 2020. *Glass: Material-Specific Data.* www.epa.gov/facts-and-figures-about-materials-waste-and-recycling/glass-material-specific-data

US Environmental Protection Agency. 2021. *Facts and Figures about Materials, Waste and Recycling.* www.epa.gov/facts-and-figures-about-materials-waste-and-recycling/national-overview-facts-and-figures-materials#Generation

Wilcox, C. 2015. Threat of plastic pollution to seabirds is global, pervasive, and increasing. *PNAS* 112(38), 11899–11904. doi: 10.1073/pnas.1502108112

World Bank Group. 2018. *What a Waste 2.0: A Global Snapshot of Solid Waste Management to 2050.* openknowledge.worldbank.org/handle/10986/30317

Acknowledgments

FROM EDUARDO:

Writing a book is a lonesome endeavor but also a team effort. In my case, I've been extremely lucky to work alongside an all-women team. This book would not be in your hands if it wasn't for my agent, Maria Whelan, who chose to believe in me when I casually pitched her the idea for "Things You Can Do" at a Brooklyn beer garden in the summer of 2019. I also owe a lot of gratitude to my editor, Sarah Malarkey, and the Ten Speed Press team, who were incredibly patient, gave sharp editorial notes, and kindly shepherded us through the intricate process of putting this jigsaw of a book together. A big thank you to all the activists, experts, and entrepreneurs who agreed to be interviewed for the profiles and to those who provided valuable insight for the manuscript, such as Robert Jones from The Nature Conservancy and Dr. Diana Ivanova from the University of Leeds. I would also like to give thanks to family and friends for cheering me on along this long, winding path during a global pandemic, especially my sister Maru, who I know will be delighted to see the book in printed form, and Valerie Hamra, who helped me relieve "book stress" during numerous Prospect Park walks. Last but not least, I have to give special thanks to Sara because I could not dream of a better ally.

FROM SARA:

First and foremost I want to thank my family and friends, especially my dear friends Lulu Watson, Julie Bernouis, Kristen Garcia, and Caroline Semmer, for a lot of emotional support and encouragement whilst I worked on *Things You Can Do* during the first Covid lockdown. I want to thank my now friend, Eduardo Garcia, for asking me to work with him on such a meaningful and well-researched project and the Ten Speed Press team for guiding us on this incredible journey. Special thanks to Liz Casella for being a supportive friend and mentor during much of my time illustrating this book and allowing me to paint in her Los Angeles design studio when everything else was shut down. Finally, I want to thank the playgrounds and outdoor spaces around Los Angeles, where I sketched many of these pages, for entertaining my child when the schools were closed.

About the Author and Illustrator

Eduardo Garcia has written news stories and features from more than a dozen countries in his more than fifteen years as a journalist. A native of Spain, Eduardo cut his teeth working as a Reuters correspondent in Guatemala, Bolivia, Argentina, Colombia, and Ecuador. Eduardo has written dozens of stories for the *New York Times* on how people can reduce their carbon footprint. Eduardo strives to lead a sustainable lifestyle and believes in using words to empower people.

Sara Boccaccini Meadows is a print designer and illustrator living in Brooklyn, New York, originally from the rolling hills of the Peak District, England. She splits her time between working as a textile designer, illustrator, and artist, using watercolor and gouache to create quirky illustrations. Sara has long been a supporter of climate action and women's rights and is dedicated to using her art to make a difference.

Index

Text copyright © 2022 by Eduardo Garcia
Illustrations copyright © 2022 by Sara Boccaccini Meadows

Library of Congress Cataloging-in-Publication Data
    Names: Garcia, Eduardo, 1976– author. | Meadows, Sara Boccaccini,
        1986– illustrator.
    Title: Things you can do : how to fight climate change and reduce waste /
        by Eduardo Garcia ; Illustrations by Sara Boccaccini Meadows
    Description: First edition. | New York : Ten Speed Press, [2022] | Includes
        bibliographical references and index.
    Identifiers: LCCN 2021031478 | ISBN 9781984859662 (trade paperback) | ISBN
    9781984859679 (ebook)
    Subjects: LCSH: Climatic changes. | Waste minimization. | Climate
        change mitigation.
    Classification: LCC QC902.8 .G37 2022 | DDC 640.28/6—dc23/
        eng/20211008
    LC record available at https://lccn.loc.gov/2021031478

Trade Paperback ISBN: 978-1-9848-5966-2
eBook ISBN: 978-1-9848-5967-9

Printed in Italy

Editor: Sarah Malarkey | Production editor: Kim Keller
Designer: Lisa Schneller Bieser
Typefaces: Filson Pro and Filson Soft by Mostardesign, Colby by J Foundry,
    Macarons by Latinotype, Palmer Lake by Jen Wagner Co.
Production manager: Dan Myers
Copyeditor: Lisa Brousseau | Proofreader: Kathy Brock
Indexer: Ken DellaPenta | Fact checker: Hannah Seo
Publicist: Felix Cruz | Marketer: Monica Stanton

10 9 8 7 6 5 4 3 2 1

First Edition